ZOMBIES DON'T SWIM

My Solar Electric Sailboat Adventures
in Puget Sound, Washington

D1738822

Charlie LaMarche

Title
Zombies Don't Swim – My Solar Electric Sailboat
Adventures in Puget Sound, Washington

ISBN 9798884563193

Cover design by Charlie LaMarche

1st Edition

Author's email: charlie@zombiesdontswim.com

Website: www.zombiesdontswim.com

Acknowledgements

To my sisters, Liz, and Becky, for reading and editing my manuscripts, and for their support in my endeavors.
To the leaders and members of Seattle Singles Yacht Club who work tirelessly to provide fun activities and a safe place for people to learn how to sail. Thanks to the skippers I served for teaching me how to sail the big boats.
To the staff members of all the marinas I have visited in the past few years. Their responsibilities range from being the harbor master to facilities managers; they were all very professional and accommodating.
And last, but not least, thanks to my liveaboard neighbors for their friendship and camaraderie, and for listening to my stories. For those former neighbors who cast off to sail the world, hope to see you out there someday!

CONTENTS

DISCLAIMER

In this book neither the publisher nor the author is engaged in rendering professional advice or services to the reader. The ideas and suggestions provided in this book are not intended as a substitute for seeking professional advice. Neither the publisher nor the author shall be held liable or responsible for any loss or damage allegedly arising from any suggestion or information contained in this book. The people I've met during this journey have had their names and identifying characteristics altered. The companion website for this book https://zombiesdontswim.com_contains a picture gallery and blog.

FOREWORD

Ever since I converted my sailboat to run on an electric inboard motor, then to a liveaboard boat and a solar-powered, off-the-grid aquatic recreational vehicle, I have had a lot of people tell me that this was also their dream; to cast off from the shore of their landlocked existence and embrace the aquatic lifestyle, with all the adventure, beauty, and serenity of the open water. Some people have the circumstances to fulfill those dreams, while others with those dreams were never able to actualize them. It takes some physical strength and stamina to sail, and a certain amount of knowledge and experience. I have read books from people who buy a sailboat and immediately set off for their adventure. Some of them succeed, others end up lost or being rescued at sea. I am a cautious person. I gained experience over several years before buying my own sailboat. I joined a yacht club and learned how to sail and navigate by volunteering to crew others' boats. I read sailing and navigation books, delved into online sailing forums, and watched a lot of YouTube videos. These things help, but don't totally prepare you to pilot your own boat. When you take your boat out of its safe berth in a marina for the first time after making major alterations, you are hyperaware of your surroundings; you begin to feel the currents trying to smash your boat into the other boats around you. Meanwhile you are trying to remember everything you are supposed to do; the 3 blasts on your horn to warn boats in the channel you are coming out from the pier. Then, when you clear the channel and enter the wide-open bay for the first time, you begin to relax and get that awesome feeling of accomplishment; all your hard work has come to fruition.

This experience changed me. You become a different person after spending days and weeks on the water, your senses engaged by the world around you; the sound of waves gently lapping against the hull at night when you are safely ensconced in your warm berth; the sound of the wind singing through your rigging, and of the rain pattering gently over your head while you are safe and dry inside. Smelling the fresh salty sea breezes and pine scented forests. You watch the gulls and kingfishers dive and scoop up their dinners, the majestic whales breaching, and the dolphins gracefully surfacing and bowing back into the sea. I have sailed at night under the moon and stars, listening to the sea lions breathing and diving around my boat while keeping me company. I opened my mind and senses and began to really understand the sea and its inhabitants.

CHAPTER 1: MY OFF-THE-GRID SOLAR ELECTRIC SAILBOAT EXPERIMENT

This is an account of my journey while repowering a sailboat with an inboard electric motor, and turning it into a tiny, solar powered electric home and aquatic recreational vehicle. I will relate to you the things I've learned and of the experiences and adventures I've had while cruising around the Puget Sound area near Seattle, Washington.

I am not an expert marine electrician or mechanic, although I am much better at those things now. I started this project with some experience remodeling homes, including plumbing, drywall, and some electrical work. When beginning a project, I would read how-to books and apply for permits as required. Inspectors who examined my work told me that I did this work just as well as professional contractors. My career was in Information Technology, which helped me with performing Internet searches, typing, and project management. I have some mechanical experience gained from working on my cars. I can change the oil and replace parts like alternators and starters. As a teenager, I rebuilt motorcycle and Volkswagen engines. They all still ran afterwards, and I survived those experiences. I also have experience assembling Christmas presents and Ikea furniture. I found out during this project; boats are completely different. The ocean's salty air and water are very corrosive, and I learned which materials are better than others for exposure to this environment. I didn't know anything about fiberglass. Any work I wasn't 100% confident of completing safely was farmed out to professionals.

I encourage anyone who wants to do their own work to do as much research as possible. Some of my most valuable information came from the American Yacht Builders Council (ABYC) for boatbuilding standards at https://abycinc.org/default.aspx. I also got great advice from Thunderstruck Motors when purchasing their electric motor kit. Their website https://www.thunderstruck-ev.com/ contains many how-to videos and technical specifications.

This project took me the better part of 3 years to complete. I did most of the work on this boat myself. Some work, like the through hull fittings, required 2 people and fiber glassing skills, so I contracted out that works. Boat mechanics can earn $90 per hour or more, depending on their specialty. Many professionals who work on boats were booked weeks and months in advance. Some boat mechanics will give you free information, but I have heard of other mechanics who will charge you $50 for each question. Once, I asked a marine upholstery contractor about making new cushions for my boat. She was booked out until the following year! Interest in boating was high during the Covid-19 pandemic because it was a safer alternative to indoor activities. Things may be different now, and it might be easier to contract out some work. I am impatient, however, and don't mind learning how to do things.

When I completed remodeling this boat, I requested a free Coast Guard safety inspection. This inspection is performed annually by Coast Guard members or authorized, experienced captains. No citations are issued during the inspection, and you get a copy of the report that you can use to remedy any deficiencies. I highly recommend this inspection. It may save lives. Also, if you are requested to stop your boat in the open water by the Coast Guard, they can penalize you for safety violations. I couldn't do everything I wanted to do to my boat before starting my off-grid life, but I ensured that my boat passed the Coast Guard safety inspection!

CHAPTER 2: DREAMS

I have always loved boating. My father, uncles, aunts, grandparents, and cousins were avid fishermen. Although I enjoyed fishing, I really loved just being on the water. Maybe because my birth sign was Pisces. I learned how to swim at a young age. As a teenager, I saved my money while working at a part-time job after school and bought a canoe. It was blue. I remember listening to a song in the lyrics of "Where to Now, St. Peter" sung by Elton John, that featured a "blue canoe" in the lyrics. My friends and I spent many hours exploring the small lakes in Arizona. We changed the lyrics from the song "Me and You and a Dog Named Boo" and sang "Me and You and a Blue Canoe". Later, I bought my first sailboat, a second-hand 9-foot Sunfish. I took the boat out to the small lakes around Tucson, Arizona. It was easy to sail, with simple controls consisting of a mainsail and a rudder. I loved going out in strong winds so I could go faster. One weekend, while camping at a lake, the summer monsoons arrived in Southern Arizona. A thunderstorm was brewing. Not a lot of lightning, but the wind started blowing, probably 30 miles an hour. I took the Sunfish out, raised the sails, and started dashing through the waves. It was bliss. Suddenly, a gust of wind caught the sail, and ripped it in half. Although I had patched the fiberglass and Styrofoam hull many times, water had got in and saturated the hull enough that it wasn't worth repairing again. Its final trip was to the landfill. The little sailboat had died, but the dream of sailing a big boat to exotic destinations lived on.

Some people get into sailing by pursuing their dreams of travelling to distant and exotic lands. Several of my former marina neighbors made their getaway last summer and have completed the first leg of their journey. They are now wintering in Mexico, while some of them are recovering from mosquito borne tropical diseases they unfortunately picked up on the trip. They are now preparing for the next step in their journeys to islands in the South Pacific. Some sailors choose to live aboard their boat while working remotely (thanks to high-speed Internet access) and prepare for their journey. Others love sailing but can't afford a house and a blue water sailboat at the same time. I encourage them to investigate liveaboard life. Your own dreams of casting off and sailing to far-off lands may be tempered by your life situation and budget. But if you are willing to put in the work, you can make your dreams come true for less money than you expect.

There were times early in the project when the work seemed never-ending. I got so tired and discouraged that I almost gave up. However, due to the Covid-19 pandemic, I didn't have anything better to do. Besides, this was my opportunity to make my dream come true. As I successfully completed a few tasks, I became more confident in my abilities. I don't regret a single minute spent in this endeavor. The scope of this project grew from a simple plan to make my boat reliable enough to sail around the bay outside of my marina, to being my off-the-grid home and environmentally responsible recreational vehicle. Someday I might sail this boat to Mexico!

CHAPTER 3: MONEY

It takes some money to realize a sailing dream, but if you make a good choice when buying a used boat and do much of the work yourself, not as much as you might expect. I spent about $25,000 altogether on my project, which includes the boat price of $5000. I was also able to take a Federal Income Tax credit for my solar power installation. (Please consult a tax attorney for this tax credit for your financial situation!). In retrospect, if I were planning to retire and live on a boat, I might have gone with a more expensive and larger boat. But I already had this one. Even if the project was a disaster and I failed abjectly, I wouldn't be out a lot of money.

I had planned a roadmap to complete the work needed. With most of the projects I made one or two false starts, accumulating knowledge along the way. I did most of the work myself and acquired some valuable skills, like soldering and low voltage electronics, especially with wire sizes, terminals, and fuses. I learned how to tie knots in rope for various purposes, and how to sew sail covers and seat cushions. The most important things I learned was to get as much information as you can in the planning stage before beginning a task, and to use marine rated components whenever possible. I hope this book illustrating my experiences helps you determine if you should take on a project like this and save you time and money if you begin your own.

CHAPTER 4: SEATTLE SINGLES YACHT CLUB

I was newly divorced when I moved to Seattle in 2012 for a new job. One of my colleagues overheard me talking about wanting to go sailing. She said, "Have I got the club for you!". I met her for a Monday evening meeting of the Seattle Singles Yacht Club (SSYC) in the ballroom of the South China Restaurant on the west shore of Lake Union. This club had been formed by single sailors who needed crew to help take their boats out. In return for the price of $15.00 for meeting dues and bringing some food for a picnic, you could learn how to sail and enjoy some time on the water. The meeting started with the officers of the club discussing business and upcoming events, then they opened the floor to skippers who advertised their open slots for boat trips. The skippers would describe their trip, where they were going, the dates, and how many volunteers they needed to crew the boat. There were both power boat and sailboat options available. The fleet captain would then hand a numbered burgee flag on a short, weighted pole to the skipper, who took it to a table. After the trip announcements were done, the prospective crew would go to the skipper's table and sign up for the trip. First-time members got to choose first, and I picked a sailing trip. Some of the skippers were picky about the food they wanted. Other skippers didn't want red wine onboard. My skipper liked roast beef and cheddar sandwiches. On the Friday evening before the trip, I made hearty roast beef sandwiches with thick slices of cheddar on bakery rolls. The next day I went down to Shilshole Marina where the skipper moored his boat. After asking and being granted permission to come aboard, the crew assembled. The skipper gave us a few basic safety rules, and then we motored out of the marina and hoisted the sails. The weather was perfect for learning how to sail. A cool day, a little overcast with a gentle breeze. It was awesome to be out sailing on this perfect day. The skipper gave us lessons as we sailed along. We learned the parts of a sailboat, how to read the ripples on the water, what the different types of buoys meant, rules of the road and boating etiquette. The crew also learned teamwork that we would use while sailing in races with other boats. Another important lesson I learned was to stick around after a trip to help clean the boat and get it ready for the next trip. This would ensure the skipper would welcome us back for another trip!

After attending several meetings and enjoying trips with other skippers, I joined SSYC as an annual member. This was a great social club that enjoyed boating. Many times after a trip, the crew would get together afterwards at a bar or restaurant and trade stories. When I was younger, I never thought I would have membership in a yacht club. As it turns out, I couldn't have completed this project without one.

CHAPTER 5: CAPTAIN ARNOLD

I became friends with a skipper by the name of Arnold. We took trips in his boat, exploring various harbors, tied up to other boats and shared food, wine, and conversation. We spent several summers this way. Arnold had lost his kidneys due to diabetes and spent a significant amount of time on dialysis. He told us that to pay for health care, he had to either give up his boat or his house. He gave up the house and moved onto the boat. Arnold had a career with an outdoor recreational goods store, and had climbed Mt. Rainier, the tallest mountain in Washington, several times. Because of his illness, by the time I met him, he could barely climb a curb from the pavement to a sidewalk. He could still sail and live the life he loved, though, with a crew to help him.

Arnold's Sailing Lessons

Arnold was a great teacher, had a wealth of knowledge in geology and engineering, and always took an opportunity to educate the crew. He showed us his hand with a missing ring finger. The finger had become caught in a block while setting the mainsail halyard. No ring, he was already divorced when this happened. His admonitions to only handle one line at a time carried extra weight because of that accident. "Do you see the red and green buoys?", Arnold asked as we left the breakwater levee at Shilshole Marina. "They mark the navigation channel. When you are going out to sea, the green one should be on your right, starboard side as you are going out to sea, and the red one should be on the left, port side. Coming back to the marina, it will be the other way around. A simple way to remember this is Red Right Return.". He told us, "If you see another boat that looks like it might cross your path, look at the horizon behind it. If there is a landmark like trees in the distance, see if the trees are going behind or ahead of the boat. If the trees are moving relative to it, we aren't on a collision course.". He called this "making trees". I have used this method while navigating to avoid collisions with other boats and haven't hit another boat yet!

Arnold continued to feed us knowledge and tips as we pulled on the halyard lines and raised the sails. "This part of Puget Sound has commercial lanes for cargo ships. It's like a highway for boats. There are buoys in the middle separating the southbound and northbound lanes. The ships will keep to the right, just as cars and trucks do on highways.". "Those ships are very fast", he continued "We will keep a lookout for them and cross the traffic lanes as quickly as possible." He then explained why bigger boats and ships have faster cruising speeds. "The top speed of a displacement boat depends on its length. You can find the optimal speed for a displacement hull like this sailboat by observing the wave coming from the bow. When that wave is the same length as the boat, we have reached hull speed.". Luckily, there is a mathematical equation for hull speed. Boats with displacement hulls can exceed hull speed, but it takes exponentially more power to go just a little faster.

"Can anybody tell me where the wind is stronger?", he asked. We all looked around. I saw a patch of water that was darker than the rest and pointed it out. "Correct," he said. The wind will stir up the water making waves that reflect the light away, so it will appear darker". While we made our way to our destination that day, Eagle Harbor, where we would tie up to other boats from the club and have a nautical party, an event termed a "raft-up", Arnold continued our education. He pointed out different buoys and beacons along the way and told us what they were for. They are like street and highway signs and formally referred to as the "U.S. Aids to Navigation System". Buoys and beacons are placed in specific locations and symbols of them are used in conjunction with nautical charts and maps to provide more information. There are many good websites that describe these navigational aids. There are even flashcards available to help a sailor to memorize them. www.quizlet.com is one of those sites.

Our friend and mentor, Arnold passed away shortly before the pandemic began. He is missed by his friends and has left his legacy with all the students who benefited from his tutelage.

CHAPTER 6: BUYING MY OWN BOAT

After sailing with the SSYC skippers for several years, on lakes, rivers, and the sea, I was ready for my own sailboat. Well, not quite ready. In Washington there are boater's education requirements. Although there are exceptions, most people here are required to study for a Washington State Boater Education Card before piloting a boat. The Washington State Parks website has the course and instructions on how to get the card. Here is a link to that website: https://boat.wa.gov/boating-information-portal/boaters-card/. I completed the free course offered by Boats US. Please check for the requirements to pilot a boat in your area.

Marinas

Before you buy a boat, I recommend checking for availability of slips for the size of boat you are considering. My boat is 30 feet LOA (Length Overall). I sometimes let my slip go during the summer to save some money, then towards fall, I start calling marinas for availability. Marinas typically have moorage available for boats 30 feet and under, depending on the time of year. Many boat owners have their boats hauled out and stored on land for the winter. Slips become harder to find for longer boats, and you may be put on a waiting list for them. Some desirable marinas have a 2-year or longer waiting list. If you buy a boat docked at a marina, the slip may be transferable. Boat mooring fees are usually charged by length plus taxes and utility charges. Catamarans are usually shorter than comparable single hull boats, so mooring charges may be less. However, they are wider, so you might have trouble finding slips wide enough. Although you should be prepared to pay first and last month's rent and deposits, it is much easier to rent a boat slip than it is to rent an apartment or house!

Where to find boats

There are yacht brokers who advertise boats online, and sailing and boating magazines have a section listing boats for sale. These boats may be well maintained but come at a premium. There are government and private salvage auction sites where you can register and bid on boats. You might be able to get a great deal on a boat there but check the rules and regulations and know what you're getting in to. There are generally additional fees and conditions. Individual marinas may have abandoned boats for auction or sale. And then there is Craigslist, where I bought my boat. There are some good books available for things to consider when buying a boat. You should read them, but here are some things I discovered while looking in the Seattle area. Boats tend to get cheaper towards the end of boating season. It can cost several hundred dollars a month to keep a boat at a marina, giving the owner incentive to let it go. I've also noticed that boats get cheaper the further away you get from civilization. For instance, a boat moored in the San Juan Islands, or the Hood Canal can be several thousand dollars less than a similar boat moored in the Seattle metropolitan area. Some people save money by buying boats in Mexico and hire a pilot and crew to bring them to Seattle. I have noticed advertisements from people selling their boat for medical reasons. These boats may be great bargains, providing the owners have kept up on the maintenance. Others may have spent many thousands of dollars rebuilding a boat but end up getting discouraged and quit. They then sell it to recover some of their loss. Others must let their sailboat go because of moving for a new job. I have seen some exquisitely beautiful wooden boats, but personally, I wouldn't buy one. Some marinas won't take them, and they can deteriorate quickly if you aren't on top of their maintenance needs. If you decide to buy a boat, in addition to researching sailing magazine reviews and boater forums, you should get a survey done. A boat survey is much like a home inspection. This gives you a good idea of the boat's condition. Knowing this up front can save you a lot of heartache and money, and gives you leverage to negotiate a better price. Finally, you will have to pay an excise tax and registration fees in Washington. Since my boat had been registered with the US Coast Guard, I was able to keep its registration number with my boat. That didn't save me any money. I applied the decal to the outside of the forward part of the cabin, but I didn't have to stencil a registration number on my hull. You can find the information for Washington at https://dor.wa.gov/education/industry-guides/vessel-brokers-and-dealers/tax-responsibilities-boat-owners.

I have heard that some boats built after the 1970's have problem with blistering or other issues due to construction methods and quality or scarcity of the epoxy resin used in their construction. While researching the sailboat forums, I have read stories of boats with blistering problems or separation of the fiberglass. My Rawson 30 has at least 1/2 inch of fiberglass everywhere. It's even thicker in places that are under a lot of stress. Although my boat is over 60 years old, the hull has always been well maintained. I haven't found any blisters or any other problems with its fiberglass. Sailors have told me that the older boats were built tough, whereas newer boats were engineered to use the least amount of fiberglass possible. You should get an insurance policy for your boat. Most every marina will require that you have at least liability insurance before renting you a slip for your boat. Consider getting towing insurance, based on your risk tolerance, the distance you travel, and number of times you might need to be towed to the nearest port. Towing policies are relatively expensive, but comparable to the price of a couple of tows.

Why Did I Choose This Boat?

I wanted a cheap, sturdy, and blue-water capable sailboat. Blue-water means a boat capable of sailing the oceans of the world from one continent to another. I spent at least a year researching and evaluating boats. I would visit online sailing forums to find opinions from experienced sailors. I watched YouTube videos of boats in different locations around the world. I read yachting magazines and online forums. I even found copies of original advertisements and specifications online. I must have tried out 15 different boats before I found "the one". After kicking tires and trying out different boats, I fell in love with a 1960 Rawson 30 sailboat. Here is its review in a historical copy by Richard Smith of Cruising World: "Ron Rawson built some of the U.S. West Coast's finest workboats—tough and able gillnetters, long-liners, and others that ply the waters between California and the Gulf of Alaska. When he decided to build sailboats, he wanted to continue the firm's reputation for building seaworthy small craft and commissioned Pacific Northwest naval architect William Garden to design the Rawson 30. Between 1959 and 1985, he built 288 Rawson 30s, of which 36 were pilothouse models. Bluff-bowed and rugged, with a long keel encapsulating 5,000 pounds of boiler punchings and concrete, the Rawson 30 was intended strictly for cruising. The hull is hand-laid solid fiberglass, while the deck is of fiberglass and balsa sandwich construction. Its bulwarks, 6 inches high at the bow, are fit for wedging in seaboots whether you're hauling in salmon or changing headsails when thrashing to windward, and its cockpit is small, as befits a blue water boat, while still adequate for two. Hardware is robust and simple.". The article mentions the "pilothouse model" which has an enclosed cockpit. I can see how it would have been nice to have that model while sailing in Seattle's rainy weather, but I reasoned that I could build a hard dodger or put up a Bimini cover later to provide some additional shelter and extend Seattle's sailing season comfortably. After watching a YouTube video of the Rawson 30 sailing in the South Pacific with a crew of 3, the boat captured my heart. As events unfolded, this boat would become the base for my off-the-grid boat project.

CHAPTER 7: MAINTENANCE BEGINS

At the exact moment the boat becomes yours, it will immediately begin falling apart. One day, I noticed the wood toe/rub rail that sits on the joint between the fiberglass deck and hull was rotting and pieces of it were falling off the boat. The previous owner had patched it with plastic wood and painted it many times, but it needed to be replaced. Its purpose is to protect the seam between the hull and deck, allow for mounting of the jib sail traveler and cars, and provides a sacrificial rub surface with the dock. You can wedge your toes under the rail for security when handling lines. Finally, it is also the last thing you can grab and hold on to while falling overboard. My initial thought was to replace it with long 2" diameter treated poplar wood dowels. I bought the wood and proceeded to cut a channel from one end of the boards to the other using a table saw. This activity was fraught with mistakes. I ruined several pieces of dowel by cutting outside the lines. Then I had the problem of cleaning up the inside of the channel so the wood would cover the seam between the deck and hull. Then I realized I would have to steam the wood to bend to the curves in the hull, and I would have to brush many coats of stain and polyurethane varnish to seal it against moisture. One of my neighbors walked by as I was dry fitting the wood. He was a shop teacher at the local high school. "What kind of wood is that?", he asked. "Poplar", I answered. "Oh, you shouldn't use that", he said, "poplar rots too easily". That got me to thinking. I went to the hardware store and started looking around at various materials I could use. I went to the lumber section of the store and found PVC trim boards for use under the eaves of a house. PVC is very weather resistant and doesn't rot. It was the perfect solution. I removed the rest of the old toe rail by taking out the screws, then filled in the screw holes with fiberglass repair compound. I then measured and cut the 20-foot 1"x2" PVC strips to fit along the top and sides of the hull joint. Then I used a marine sealant by the 3M company. It was the 5200 sealant and according to their website it was advertised for: "VERSATILE APPLICATIONS: Tough yet flexible polyurethane polymer is ideal for deck housings, hull fittings, porthole mounting, fiberglass transoms, and underside molding". Although this sealant is rather pricy, I used it liberally on the top and sides of the hull joint. Then I clamped the rails in place and drilled new holes for the top and side screws. I used stainless steel #12 screws, 1 1/2" for the top, and 2-1/4" for the side so they would go through the hull and secure the outside rail. This was a perfect solution. The PVC is easy to keep clean; it's tough, flexible, and durable. After 4 years, I have only had one problem with the rub rail; during a storm while tied up at a dock, the mooring lines and fenders smashed against the rail repeatedly, shattering a segment of it. It was easily replaced and repaired. I reasoned that the same thing would have happened to teak wood rails, and they would have been more expensive and harder to replace. I have since used PVC pipe and fittings to replace the rotting grab rail and luggage rack on the roof of my boat; they have proved to be sturdy and have passed the test of time. I saved so many hours of work and a lot of money by using PVC instead of teak.

CHAPTER 8: THROUGH HULL PLUMBING

The through hulls are bronze, brass, or stainless-steel plumbing fittings that pass through a hull and are generally below the waterline. They are connected inside the hull to a ball valve with a lever you can use to close it and keep water from coming in or going out. If the valve is open and you get a leak in a hose attached to it, sea water can come into the boat. If the boat's automatic bilge pump can't pump out all the water coming in, your boat can sink. One Saturday, as I was re-routing hoses from the cockpit drain, I discovered that a couple of through hull valves were stuck in the open position. I made a mental note to have those valves replaced and left to go home. The next morning as I was getting ready to go back to the boat, my phone rang. It was a marina staff member calling because my bilge pump had been running continuously, pumping water out of the boat. He took the initiative to inspect the boat and stop the leak. He told me that one of the hoses was so old and brittle, it had cracked. On my way to the boat, I stopped at a marine supply store and picked up some 3/4" flexible, reinforced vinyl tubing. After I repaired the plumbing, I called a marine mechanic to replace the through hull fittings, who subcontracted a fiberglass specialist, then made an appointment with a boat yard for a haul out. On the designated morning, a Friday, I took the boat for the 2-mile journey to the boatyard. The boatyard staff told me I had to contact an operator to raise the bridge because it was too low for my sailboat's mast to pass under. I could either use channel 13 on the VHF radio or call via phone. As I approached the bridge, I used the VHF radio to make the call. The operator acknowledged and quickly raised the bridge. This was my first bridge transit and the first time I made a call via radio! After docking the boat at the haul out area, I walked up the hill to a safe observation point and watched the proceedings. The haul out process was interesting. A huge forklift machine with 2 heavy duty straps approached my boat and the forks slipped the straps under my boat. The forklift operator lifted my 6-ton boat smoothly out of the water and backed up the ramp. He then slowly drove around the corner of the garage, where another employee pressure washed the bottom and sides of the boat. The bottom paint on boats contains chemicals to repel critters that would try to build their homes on it. The chemicals are eventually used up or leach out of the paint, so the longer you leave a boat in the water, the more animal and plant life will grow on it. My boat's previous owner had hauled the boat every few years, so the hull didn't have a lot of growth on it. Before too long, the forklift trundled my boat carefully to its dry dock space. I was still working at the time, so I couldn't watch my contractors do the through hull installation. They only took a couple of half-days to complete their work, including the installation of the new valves, fiberglass work and re-connecting the plumbing. There are two parts of the bronze through hull fittings, one male threaded fitting with a flange that goes through the hull and another part that looks like a mushroom cap that screws on from the outside of the hull to secure it. The mechanic was shocked to find that the boat was constructed with only the inside fitting screwed into the hull. It didn't have the external mushroom part. Over the 60 years this boat was in the water, all it would have taken was a sharp tap to dislodge the fitting, allowing the ocean to infiltrate the boat! Now might be a good time to make a checklist of maintenance items you need to perform on a regular basis. Because most of the through hull valves need to be left open to drain water from the scuppers and cockpit, they need to be exercised occasionally to make sure they will shut off as needed. Check and replace your flexible hoses and replace them if they are deteriorating.

The price of the haul out was $700 for the week, and the cost for the mechanics was $400. It was money well spent.

A Note About Boatyards and Haul Out Providers

While I have heard horror stories about boats being damaged or even dropped during the haul out process, I assume that is the exception rather than the rule. When selecting a boatyard for your hull work, you might want to get references or read their reviews. This would also be a good time to ensure that your insurance covers accidental damages!

CHAPTER 9: NEW BOTTOM PAINT

Since the mechanics finished the project early, I decided to spend my weekend sanding the hull and applying new bottom paint. This needs to be done every three or four years, so I thought I would take care of it now rather than later. The previous owner left me supplies, including 2 gallons of antifouling paint. This paint prevents marine life from making their home on your boat's hull. If left untreated, your boat would eventually become a reef. The Washington State Department of Ecology has been concerned with the use of copper, which is the active ingredient of many antifouling paints, because it is harmful to fish and other marine life. They are working with the University of Washington to find a viable alternative to copper in antifouling paint. There are many regulations for boat repair facilities that were made to keep harmful substances from polluting the land and water. When working on your boat in a boatyard, be sure to read the regulations and obey the shipyard staff. This example from Swantown Marina highlights best practices around boat maintenance: https://swantown.portolympia.com/wp-content/uploads/sites/2/2020/08/best-management-practices.pdf. Boat maintenance facilities strictly adhere to these practices and are inspected regularly. I use a dive service to regularly inspect my boat. The diver will examine the hull and propeller, check the knot meter paddle wheel and depth finder transducer, and give the hull a light cleaning. The diver will also replace the "zincs" on your propeller and shaft. The water acts as an electrolyte, like the fluid in a battery. "Zincs" are sacrificial anodes that are attached to the expensive metal parts of your boat and will be eaten away by the electro-chemical action first. The scientific reason is because zinc is more reactive than nobler metals (remember the periodical table in chemistry?) and attracts and consumes corrosive electrons, while sacrificing tiny pieces of itself. The diver will also let me know when the boat's antifouling paint starts failing. Back at the boatyard, I spent my weekend, two 12-hour days, sanding and applying the new antifouling paint. I let it dry for a few days, and then my boat was ready to drop back into the water. I took Friday off from work to motor the boat back to the marina, very satisfied with the work that had been done to it. I could rest easy knowing my boat wouldn't sink anytime soon!

CHAPTER 10: MAST STEPS

On occasion, you may need to perform maintenance at the top of the mast. That is where a sailboat's all-around light, the VHF radio antenna, the anemometer, which measures windspeed, and the windvane are located. At times, you may need to get up there to replace a lightbulb or you might need to adjust the wings of the windvane according to how your boat tacks. You can hire a rigger to perform this work, or you can do it yourself. I wanted to learn how to climb the mast. It might come in handy if I had an emergency on the water. There are several ways to reach the top of the mast. The monkey grinder method is when a small person is strapped into a Bosun's chair attached to a halyard and hoisted up by a larger person on the deck turning a crank. One of my neighbors volunteered to be the "small person", but he got cold feet on the day we set to do it. There are different climbing aids; one is foot straps that are snugged on a rope, where you can climb the rope by lifting one foot up, anchoring it, and then slide the other foot up. Another way is to use a rope ladder. I tried that method, but any movement of the boat is amplified by the mast, and it gets scary quickly. I ended up buying and installing folding foot pegs to the mast. They are made from high strength plastic and are attached by drilling small holes in the mast and using aluminum rivets to secure them. That was hard work and took a few days to complete, but I gained another skill by using the rivets. I'm very happy with these steps. Not only can I reach the top of the mast, but I used them once while anchored out on the water to re-attach a spreader that was torn off in a windstorm! Although I didn't need anybody's help while climbing up the mast to install the steps, I took some comfort that my neighbor across the pier kept an eye on me. She would worry about me while I was 20 feet off the deck. "Charlie, you're nuts for climbing up there!", she exclaimed, "But I'll call 911 if you fall." It is so good to have neighbors like that!

CHAPTER 11: THE COVID-19 PANDEMIC

I took notice of the Covid-19 virus when residents at a nursing home in Kirkland, Washington became ill. I lived in Kirkland when I started working in downtown Seattle for a fashion retailer company. I moved away from Kirkland, though, in 2018 due to the increasing commute time for my job in Seattle. I commuted either by car or bus. The commute by car was easy in the morning, but by evening became a 2 hour stop and go nightmare. Public transport was the same, not too bad in the morning, but by the time evening rolled around, some people became rude; shoving and pushing each other for a spot on the bus, not wanting to wait 20 minutes for the next bus on the route. We were packed into the bus, our bodies wedged against others, literally like sardines in a can. The public transportation experience can be dehumanizing. Having enjoyed taking some trips on the ferry boats, I decided to move to Bremerton, Washington, on the west side of Puget Sound. Housing was cheaper there, and the commute to Seattle by ferry took about the same amount of time that I was spending on the bus from Kirkland. On the ferry, however, you had enough space to stretch out on the bench seats and nap. After catching the morning ferry, which left at 5:20 AM, most of my fellow passengers slept, getting another 40 winks in before starting their working day. In the afternoon trip back across the Puget Sound, one could stroll around the deck, taking in the beautiful scenery and fresh ocean air. In Bremerton, I was never infected with the virus and felt fortunate to be living far from the epicenter of a Covid-19 breakout.

The Pandemic Layoffs

I took a week off from my job in late March 2020 for a vacation with my mother and siblings in Hawaii. This would be my mother's last trip. At 83 years old, she had been diagnosed with stage 4 lung cancer. Upon returning to Bremerton, my boss called and told me to stay at home. Our company, a fashion retailer, had temporarily closed all their stores due to the Covid-19 pandemic. We were to work from home until further notice. Six weeks later, I and a cohort of my Information Technology colleagues were laid off. I was able to spend more time with my mother in her last few days, and my sailboat remodeling project was suddenly prioritized.

Zombies Don't Swim

In the beginning of the Covid-19 pandemic, people were panicking and raiding big box stores for enough supplies to last until the health crisis was resolved; there were news stories and videos of folks fighting over toilet paper. What was the reason given for the fights over toilet paper? "Well, there wasn't much left, and everybody else was buying it!". Luckily, I had stocked up on paper products and bottled water a few weeks earlier. So, I made my own trip to the big box stores and bought enough canned and dry goods to last for a few months. Because there was so much uncertainty about the virus and its morbidity, I took the supplies down to my boat, and made it ready to cast off. This would be my "go" boat. If the pandemic turned out to be an apocalypse, I could sail my boat out into the middle of Puget Sound. Zombies don't swim! No, really, I looked it up! Because they are so uncoordinated, they can't swim. They can walk of course, but if the water around is too deep for them to stand and reach your boat, you will be safe.

CHAPTER 12: MOTHER EARTH NEWS

I was a teenager in 1973 when the oil crisis and gasoline shortages impacted the United States. I wasn't old enough to drive, but I remember riding my bicycle around and seeing cars lining the streets for blocks, waiting to get gas. Fuel was rationed. People waited in lines for hours, only for the filling stations to run out of gas. As they drove away to find another gas station, the attendant hung a cardboard sign. "Out of Gas", it said.

My parents were scientists. My father was a climatologist who worked with tree rings. He sometimes took me for field trips into the forests in the Sierra Nevada mountains in California, and I would help him to gently take core samples from the very old trees that grew there. Some of those trees were nearly 5,000 years old. Then he brought the samples to the lab, where he and other scientists would cut thin slices of the narrow straw-like cores lengthwise, take slide photos of them, and match them up in their database. I still remember looking at those slides on the view screen and the pine rosin smell from the wood core repository. They made records from these trees that dated back thousands of years, and they could tell how much rainfall or snow fell in a particular season of the year, and how the climate was changing from one century to another. Using this chronology, or timeline, they could further validate carbon-14 dating and determine the age of timbers used in boats or structures down to the year they were made. In 1984 he and some colleagues wrote an article for Nature Magazine about rising CO_2 levels and temperatures and their effects on tree growth. Scientists knew back then that humans were contributing to a changing climate. One of my father's career highlights was helping Carl Sagan produce a television show about the climate effects that an atomic war would have by extrapolating the effects that volcanic eruptions had in the past. The bombs would throw up so much dust into the upper atmosphere, it would turn the earth into a giant snowball. Hence the term "nuclear winter". It's ironic that humanity is now concerned about hotter temperatures. My mother was an archaeologist and taught me how the First Nations people built their homes to capture heat during the day in thick walls that would radiate heat back into the interior of the house on cold desert nights. My parents kept bookshelves stocked with a huge assortment of books and magazines. Because I had seen the effects of energy shortages first-hand, I became keenly interested in renewable energy and the environment. I would pore over Mother Earth News magazine articles, learning about renewable energy and alternative lifestyles. Later, when I bought my first house, I built a working solar water heater for it. This was a good project for Arizona where anything left out in the sun would get hot. Since this house was constructed of adobe bricks, it only needed a simple evaporative air conditioner to keep the interior cool during the hot desert summer days. Although my career and life took me in a different direction, I always believed that renewable energy would help save humanity and this planet. And now, because solar and wind energy is now cheaper to produce than fossil energy, many countries like Australia, Chile, and Honduras have invested in it. Those countries are now meeting nearly all their electricity demand using renewable energy sources. If they can, why can't the US?

Recycling and Housing

By rebuilding a 60-year-old fiberglass boat, I am helping the environment by recycling tons of material that would otherwise end up in a landfill, or as a derelict stranded on a shoal somewhere, leaking fuel, sludge, and other contaminants into the water. By replacing the boat's gasoline engine with an electric motor my lifestyle is becoming more carbon neutral. It occurred to me while living on this boat and making it my home, that I was issuing myself a mandate to reduce my energy and water consumption. I also de-cluttered my life significantly. On a boat, you are physically constrained; there is a limited amount of space available. I would have to use every nook and cranny in the cabin, under the cockpit, and on the deck, for supplies, cooking utensils, food and water. There would have to be a hierarchy for the things I needed most to be at hand. Weight was a consideration. The boat needed to be balanced, with most of the weight below the waterline and as close to the keel as possible. Later, while ensconced in my snug little home, it occurred to me that I was freeing up housing elsewhere for someone else to live in!

CHAPTER 13: PLANNING AND ENGINEERING

When I planned the conversion of my 30-foot sailboat into an off-the-grid camping and recreational vehicle, I had no doubt that the project would succeed. This was my chance to finally realize my dreams of sailing, while incorporating renewable energy. I had all the incentive I needed to overcome any obstacles. I couldn't plan for everything; many of the things I needed to do, I had never done before. I made mistakes along the way, but as I overcame each setback, I grew more confident in my ability to figure things out. I learned so much from this project and from the people around me, my neighbors, friends, marina staff, yacht club members, and from the employees at the hardware and marine stores.

House Batteries

My boat has eight Group 27 12-volt deep cycle batteries that store electricity from the solar panels for the boat's house power system. There are two sets of 4 batteries, connected in parallel. I wired in an A/B switch to disconnect the electricity while working on the circuits, and to switch to a different set of batteries in case one bank was depleted. This 12-volt system includes the navigation system, VHF radio, lighting, and a 3000-watt pure sine wave inverter. Although could have bought more expensive 12-volt RV appliances for my boat, I decided to go with cheaper conventional appliances. The inverter powers a dorm room size refrigerator, microwave oven, entertainment center, and my laptop computer. During the summer, with the long days and dry weather, I have all the power I need. Unfortunately, during the cloudy Pacific Northwest winters with its shorter daylight hours, I must prioritize my electricity use accordingly. To keep the refrigerator running, I use the microwave oven less often; instead of using the entertainment center with the big screen TV, DVD player, and powered speakers, I use my laptop and headphones for video and music. I have a propane tank onboard, my concession to fossil fuels. In the winter I use propane for cooking and pre-heating the cabin before retiring at night. The propane gas is turned on by using a solenoid switch, which is a USCG safety requirement. However, I turn the propane off at night. Even though my propane heater has a low oxygen sensor shutoff system, and I have carbon monoxide detectors on board, I don't trust having propane on while I sleep. I have an electric mattress pad that doesn't use much electricity, and the insulated cabin keeps me plenty warm at night.

Drive Batteries

The electricity for the drive motor uses four Group 31 and four Renogy 200ah AGM batteries, also on an A/B switch, for the inboard electric drive motor. These two sets of four batteries are wired in series to produce 48 volts. I use the A/B switch to disconnect power when performing wiring work, and for switching between the sets. There are also two separate AGM batteries wired in series for the 24v 80 lb. thrust trolling motor mounted on the stern. When I researched the high capacity 200ah AGM batteries, the Renogy brand looked like the best bet. I shopped around for them, and found they were cheaper from Amazon than they were on Renogy's web site. Not to mention the free Prime shipping! I also found a bargain on the trolling motor in the scratch and dent cave at Cabela's. Since it was a bow mount marine motor with a long shaft, it was ideal for use on a sailboat, where the sides of the hull are much higher than on a fishing boat. I wanted to mount the trolling motor so I could reach it from the cockpit, so I made a new motor mount with parts from an outboard mount and attached it securely to the stern. This motor serves as a side thruster that I use for docking in confined spaces and gives me a plan "C" option for propulsion if I were to lose the main drive during adverse wind conditions. The trolling motor also works great when fishing for salmon.

Weight Distribution

While planning the repower project, I considered the weight of the battery propulsion system against that of the gasoline engine system. The electric motor and controller weighed 30 lbs., and the 8 drive batteries weighed 760 lbs., for a total of 790 lbs. The Atomic 4 engine weighed 330 lbs., and the 37-gallon gasoline tank and fuel were another 240 lbs. for a total of 670 lbs. I then added its starting batteries, for another 130 lbs., which made the total gasoline propulsion system 800 lbs. I was satisfied with that comparison of the gasoline and electric propulsion system. I would be adding 400 lbs. of batteries for the solar electricity system but considering the original net weight of the boat was 12000 lbs., the extra 400 lbs. wasn't that significant. I would mount the batteries as low as possible to make the boat more stable when navigating and sailing. I have seen boats sailing in Commencement Bay outside of Tacoma, Washington, that waffle violently from side to side at the slightest breath of wind. It occurred to me that the owner may have removed much of the keel to increase the boat's speed for racing in Seattle's mild summer winds. Someday, I might remove part of the concrete ballast in this boat's keel to make it a little lighter. If I get bored.

CHAPTER 14: THE PROJECT BEGINS

I bought the Rawson 30 before the Covid-19 pandemic began. Although I spent some time making the boat safe and reliable enough to take sailing, I didn't like the Atomic 4 engine. It didn't have any pollution controls and it mixed the exhaust with hot water from the heat exchanger and spewed it out the back. There wasn't a lot of extra room in the engine compartment, so I had to contort myself to perform routine maintenance. I changed the sparkplugs and the impeller that circulated the water in the heat exchanger. Everything on the engine that wasn't covered in paint or grease was rusted. Sometimes I would accidentally cut my hand on something sharp, and my blood would mix with the grease. After the maintenance, I took the boat out a few times to go sailing.

Oil and Fuel Spills

Occasionally, when walking down the pier to my boat, I saw diesel or gasoline sheens on the surface of the water. They had all the colors of a rainbow. Sometimes the smell of the gasoline spills was so strong, I was afraid the water would catch on fire. Whenever I saw a spill, I reported it to the marina staff. They would try to track the fuel to whichever boat was leaking it. If it was coming from a boat in our marina, they would put hydrophobic oil absorbing containment booms around the boat and notify the owner to fix the problem. Most of the time, however, the marina staff were unable to trace the leak, and while you could smell the gas or diesel, it had dispersed too much to be contained. I learned that if you saw a fuel spill, whether it was from your boat or from another source, you were bound by law to report it. You could even be punished for not reporting a spill. Information for the Washington State Department of Environment can be found at: https://ecology.wa.gov/footer-pages/report-an-environmental-issue/report-a-spill. I never saw a hazmat team or a representative from the Department of Ecology. I assumed that the small amount of oil leaked wasn't enough to warrant their attention. I also learned that you should not use liquid soap or detergent on oil spills. That just makes the oil clump together and sink, causing more problems underwater. The lighter components of petroleum will evaporate into the air, and eventually even blobs of oil are biodegradable. Because those spills really made an impression on me, I decided then that I would eventually repower the boat with a cleaner engine, for the sake of the creatures that live in the sea.

My Homebuilt Electric Bicycle

To commute from the Bremerton-Seattle ferry to my office in downtown Seattle, I rode my bicycle a mile and a half uphill to my office. One day an electric bike passed me. I thought how much faster and easier my commute would be if I had an electric bike. The bike that had passed me looked expensive. I caught a glimpse of the brand as it passed by. It was indeed over $4000. So, I found an electric hub motor kit for around $700, and in the space of a weekend, converted my bike to electric. It worked great! Because I started with a lightweight hybrid mountain bike, and the rear wheel had an 8-speed sprocket, I left the other electric bikes in the dust. The bike took a little more maintenance because of the higher speeds, and I had to replace the brake pads monthly.

Lightbulb Turns On!

Because I successfully completed an electric repower project on my bicycle, electrifying the boat was a logical next step. I reasoned that I only needed enough power to get out into the bay to catch the wind. I would replace the old, rusty, polluting Atomic 4 engine with a clean electric motor. Just thinking about helping the environment and all the time I would be sailing instead of maintaining an old, polluting engine, made this ambitious project worthwhile.

Thunderstruck Motors

I searched the Internet for marine electric motor kits and conversion offerings, and found a company called Thunderstruck Motors. They had been in business for a good long time and sold electric motor kits for cars and sailboats. They had a range of kits available for various sailboat sizes. I went to their website and started reading. There was a plethora of information about their products and even videos of ordinary people installing their kits. A lot of other sailboat electric conversion vendors recommend that their mechanics perform the installation, but Thunderstruck Motors encouraged anyone with mechanical experience to do their own conversion. I called their office, and they were very helpful and knowledgeable about their products. They were familiar with the Atomic 4 and asked me questions about my propeller and shaft size. Based on the size of my boat, my budget, and the cool Seattle climate, we settled on the air cooled 48-volt 10 kWh motor kit. I could have gone with a 72-volt, water-cooled system, but the higher voltage required installation by a licensed electrician. The kit came with a Sevcon 4 voltage controller, keyed off/ on switch, OBD connector, electronic throttle, and all the parts needed for installation, but you needed to make your own motor mount. Because the boat had a 3 bladed prop, I added a 2 to 1 transmission that used a toothed rubber belt drive. The owner of my boat had upgraded the propeller shaft from 7/8" to 1" and changed from a two-blade prop to a three-blade propeller with a 10" diameter x 7.4" pitch. Based on the RPM and torque curve for their 10kW electric motor, the folks at Thunderstruck recommended a 2:1 transmission. In retrospect, I wish I had learned more about propellers. However, this setup drives my boat close to the published hull speed of 6.3 knots, or about 7 mph. Here is more information regarding sizing the propeller: http://www.youboat.net/boatPower4.aspx. Gasoline engines are picky about their RPMs and power curves when driving a propeller, whereas an electric motor has a smoother power and torque curve. Docking a boat with an electric engine is so much easier because you can gradually take the propeller speed to 0 RPMs, and there is no shifting back and forth to accommodate for a gas engine that won't operate much below 500 RPMs.

Electric Motor Maintenance

Fortunately, sailboats don't use a lot of fuel, whereas cabin cruiser can use many gallons of fuel per hour. Gasoline or diesel motors always require some maintenance. They are complicated and can require professionals to keep them running. If you repower your boat with a 3-phase brushless electric motor, you will save a lot of time and money on engine maintenance. These motors only have a few moving parts, the shaft, and sealed bearings. The only maintenance they need is to replace the rubber drive belt occasionally, and to ensure the electrical connections are solid and clean. I looked up the duty cycle of my electric motor. It will run 10,000 hours on average. I would have to run that motor 8 hours per day for three and a half years before it would wear out. These motors are not that expensive compared to gas or diesel engines. A new motor would cost between $400 and $600, and you can replace them yourself in an hour. I'm in my 4th year with my electric motor. It's running strong, and the original rubber belt is still good.

Lifting the Atomic 4 Out of the Engine Compartment

The next step was to remove the old Atomic 4. This engine

weighed about 330 lbs., but I would take off parts of the engine, like the starter and alternator, and anything else I could and bring it down to around 200 pounds. Then I would pull it out using a chain hoist and my boom. I read articles and posts on forums from sailors using their boom to pull engines. After all, the masts on big sailboats can withstand thousands of pounds of stress from the wind. Per the Thunderstruck video tutorial, I measured the position of the shaft and wired it securely so it would stay in its original position while removing the engine. After 3 hours of battling with the motor, I had it sitting on the cockpit seat. I took a break and pondered on how to get the engine into the cart on the dock. There was a possibility that the engine would be overcome by gravity and fall into the water beneath my slip. Luckily, just then, a couple of beefy neighbors walked by and asked me if I needed help. They picked up the motor, dropped it in the cart and wheeled it up the ramp to my car. Problem solved. I could have sold the old motor. Someone would have rebuilt it and powered another boat with it. But I did the right thing and took it straight to the scrap metal yard where it couldn't do any more harm.

Installing the Electric Motor

Installation was a breeze. I made a motor mount and framework to attach the motor, transmission, and controller. To start with, just to get me out into the bay to sail, I bought four 12-volt 125 amp-hour AGM deep cycle batteries and wired them in series. I bought two 2-bank chargers and wired the terminals to each battery. I charged the batteries up, turned the power key on, and bench tested the new electric motor there at my slip. It was very quiet, just a whirring sound (kind of like a Tesla) as opposed to the gasoline engine's loud burble, and best of all, no smoke or foul stench from the exhaust! I looked over the aft rail, and I could see the prop pushing water behind the boat.

First Test Drive with the Electric Motor

The boat was ready for its first test drive! With my heart in my throat, and the US tow boat number on speed dial, I drove through the rows of boats in my marina and headed out. Everything worked great on the trial run!

Solar Panels

Because I was planning to spend some time at anchorages during the summer, I bought and installed solar panels to recharge batteries while off the grid. I made a frame out of PVC pipe that I attached to the new PVC roof rack. The solar electricity kits were from Harbor Freight. They were the cheapest and handiest option at the time. These were made with amorphous silicon cells, which, according to articles I read, were more efficient in cloudy weather. The solar power controllers had USB ports for charging my cell phone and other electronic devices. And because I added the solar panels to my project, I was able to take a Federal Income Tax credit of 30% of the total cost of the solar panels, batteries, controllers, power management systems, and wiring components! (Be sure to check with your tax advisor to see how this tax credit applies to you). I later found a great deal on polycrystalline silicon solar cells, a flexible sheet that pulls in 1000 watts from the sun and added it to the mix. I measured 7 amps of power coming from it one sunny day. It charges the boat's large AGM deep-cycle batteries within a couple of days!

A Quick Note About Power Inverters

I thought it would be handy to use household appliances while I was off the grid. So, I bought a relatively inexpensive 3000 watt modified sine wave inverter to change the boat's 12-volts direct current into 115-volts alternating current for the microwave, refrigerator, a laptop computer, tv and stereo. The forementioned appliances worked OK on the modified sine wave inverter, although the microwave gave off a buzzing sound. I also had an electrical heated mattress pad. I used it to keep warm while docked at the marina. It kept me warm enough in my well-insulated boat that I didn't need to turn on a heater except on the colder nights. It didn't use much current, so I could also use it while on the hook. Unfortunately, the first time I plugged in the mattress pad with the modified sine wave inverter, the thermostat control fried instantly with a puff of smoke. I quickly unplugged it, but the acrid fumes wafted around the boat and set off the cabin smoke detector. I decided to save up my money and get the more expensive pure sine wave inverter. And another electric mattress pad. I mounted the new inverter in a dry and accessible place in the cabin and made special plugs for it so I could plug it into the main panel box and use the AC circuit breakers. The microwave sounded better, and I'm sure my other appliances are happier with the pure sine wave power they are now receiving. I mentioned before that this book would save you time and money. You will if you don't make the same mistakes I made!

Total Cost and the Federal Income Tax Credit for Solar on Your House or RV

The cost for the motor kit and 4 new deep cycle batteries including tax was $6138 without solar. I bought Harbor Freight solar power kits because they came with controllers and wiring needed to connect to battery storage. They seemed like a good deal. I spent around $600 for them and miscellaneous switches, fuses, and supplies. I included the cost of one of the power inverters at $380. In the end, I was able to take the 30% Solar energy federal income tax credit on most of the components for $1800. (Check with your tax consultant for this credit as it applies to your situation).

The Seattle Singles Yacht Club Electric Repower Presentation

My yacht club often arranges for speakers to join our meetings and give nautically oriented presentations. When the fleet captain at SSYC heard about my sailboat repowering project, the yacht club invited me to do a presentation on repowering a boat from fossil fuel to electricity. Although this was my first presentation ever, outside of work, I wasn't at all nervous. I had prepared a speech and a slide show presentation. Because the audience was warm and I knew the material well, the speech went very smoothly. I flipped through the slides and didn't have to refer to the paper copy of the speech at all. There were around 80 people in the audience. They were all boaters, and some of them were even engineers. I was so happy that my presentation generated a lot of interest and that I was able to answer so many intelligent questions!

Off-grid Electrical Summary

The solar electric system has been operational since June 2020. As I ventured out into the Sound for longer and farther trips, and learned more about the tides and conditions in the marine environment my equipment was operating in, I upgraded to a set of four Renogy 200ah and a second set of four 130ah batteries for the drive motor and an A/B switch to change between battery sets as they become depleted. I added an ammeter to the drive circuit so I could monitor the power draw in real time. To increase efficiency, and to lessen the risk of wires overheating, I made custom oversized 2/0 marine wire cables and replaced the original #2 car battery cables for the drive batteries. I have motored some good distances with the new battery set and estimate a 60-mile range before recharging, while running conservatively at 4 knots. In case of a scenario with no wind and the drive batteries depleted, I have the 80 lb. thrust saltwater trolling motor to give me a few more miles to moor in a safe place. I haven't had any problems with the electric drive system yet. It requires very little maintenance. There is a grease fitting on the transmission I fill twice a year. The 3-phase alternating current motor is brushless, so there are no brushes to wear out. There are a few bearings around the motor shaft, but they are sealed with no maintenance required. The estimated service life of this motor is 10,000 hours. It might last me the rest of my life! I check the transmission belt drive frequently and adjust it occasionally. I have put several hundred miles on the original belt, but it shows no sign of cracking or aging. I keep a spare belt on board, but I haven't had to use it yet. Each time I turn the key, I hear the click of the solenoid and see the meter lights flash. This boat is ready to go, so I untie from the dock and silently pull out into the channel. The boat is so quiet, sometimes I have pulled into a marina slip and tied up. Then, hours later, my neighbors will step out of their cabin with an astonished look, "I didn't hear you pull in!", they say. I smile, "I get that a lot".

Remodeling the Cabin

Now that I had a boat that could travel from one anchorage to another, I wanted to remodel the interior of the boat and make it a comfortable place to live in, as if it were a floating tiny house. The previous owner had lived in the boat for 20 years. He was a nice man but wasn't very good with plumbing or wiring. When I started examining his work, I found that his answer to plumbing leaks was to put more silicone sealant on the fittings. Also, he thought painter's tape would insulate 115 volts AC wiring. I decided to strip the interior down to the hull and start over. While doing that, I started conceptualizing and planning the interior remodel. Please see the gallery photos on the companion website for this book at https://zombiesdontswim.com.

Wiring for 115 Volt AC Shore Power

I calculated my appliance's power draw. I would only need 30-amp service. Most marinas provide a 30 and/or 50-amp outlet for boat's shore power needs. I bought and installed marine grade tinned stranded copper wire, ground fault circuit interrupter (GFCI) outlets that are required for use in damp or wet locations, and a panel box with circuit breakers for the

115-volt alternating house electrical current. For the exterior plug connection, I bought a marine adapter plate which was a receptacle that would be mounted in a safe place on the hull. I wired 2–15-amp circuits, one on each side of the boat, and protected against shocks by the GFCI outlets. I checked out other boats at the marina to see where their shore power marine adapter plates were mounted and decided to install mine aft of the starboard bench seat in the cockpit. I bought a new 40-foot 30-amp rated marine power cord that had a little green light to show when the power was turned on. A few days after finishing this work, I heard shouts ringing out near me. I poked my head out to see what was happening. A fire had broken out on a boat 6 piers from me. The flames were so hot, they caught the boat next to it on fire before the fire crews could get to it. Once you get fiberglass hot enough to burn, it burns well! The marina staff and fire marshal inspected the remains of the boat. Someone had cut and spliced two cords to make a longer one and had used wire nuts and electrical tape to make the connections. The connections had oxidized quickly in the ocean air, while the wire nuts had loosened, causing resistance which in turn caused the fire. Afterwards, the marina management put out a newsletter article reminding boat owners of the proper way to attach shore power to their boats and began inspecting all the boats in the marina for compliance. I think fate speaks to those who will listen. I was proud of my new wiring job, and it passed inspection.

Wiring for 12 Volt DC

I then redesigned the 12-volt DC boat circuits. The original wiring had been done correctly with tinned copper stranded wiring that was embedded into the fiberglass hull. I tested the resistance of these wires with a circuit tester to ensure that there were no bad spots in them. I bought and installed a new marine direct current circuit panel and fuses for all the mobile appliances like the VHF radio, depth finder, bilge pumps, navigation lights, and interior lighting. All my lighting needs would be supplied by LED's that were wired into the boat's 12-volt circuits. It's amazing to see how versatile LED lights have become. In addition to their low power draw, they now produce very natural looking soft white light.

I learned so many new things while doing the low-voltage wiring. I learned how to crimp terminals onto wires, solder, and how to use a heat gun to shrink insulation around the terminals. I learned how to calculate wire size based on the distance and anticipated load for the circuit. And how important it is to match fuses to the wire size in the circuits. I built battery boxes for all the 12-volt AGM batteries. When the Coast Guard representative inspected my boat, he remarked on how clean the wiring layout was, and how sturdy the battery boxes and frames were. After several dicey situations on the water involving huge wakes from ferries, none of the batteries have budged.

Plumbing

Boat plumbing can range from simple to very complex. My boat's plumbing is on the simple side, compared to what you find in houses and more luxurious boats. Some boats have "water makers" that remove salt and impurities from ocean water. I will install one before I go on any long ocean trips. I don't have a shower yet, but I plan to remodel my small bathroom and put one in. Although you can buy small electric hot water heaters or propane instant hot water heaters, I will try to design a solar powered hot water heater. It could be built into the underside of the solar panels, serving a dual purpose of transferring heat away from the silicon cells making them more efficient at generating electricity while making warm water for the shower.

The most critical part of the plumbing on a boat is the through hull valves. These valves were frozen open on my boat; an unsafe condition since a leaking hose or pipe could sink the boat. As previously mentioned, I commissioned a team of two boat mechanics to replace the valves when the boat was in dry dock. When they were done, I used 3/4" flexible reinforced tubing to reconnect the scupper drains and the automatic bilge pump. I added another manually operated electrical bilge pump in case the automatic one failed or the boat were to be swamped. I also installed a hand operated pump; you can't be too safe.

Insulation and Headliner

Back at my slip, I continued the interior remodel. The inside of the hull, the bulkheads and built in shelves were covered in old decrepit paneling, and the owner had insulated the hull with a layer of neoprene, the same material used by wetsuits. My decorating philosophy is that form follows function. So, I removed everything from the inside of the boat that wasn't functional. While performing this work, I began formulating a plan for the new interior. I wanted a good layer of insulation to reduce condensation and make the boat more comfortable in cold weather. I sanded the original built in shelves and bulkhead walls. Then I used Killz primer paint to even out the color of the surface, then put on a coat of high-quality latex paint. I chose a light green/aquamarine paint color. Something that would remind me of land if I were far from the coast. Some of the boat's wiring ran along the inside of the hull and the underside of the deck. It occurred to me that I could make wall and ceiling panels that could be removed individually if I needed to access the hull wall. So instead of having to remove and destroy a huge section of wall to get to the hull, I would only have to remove a small piece. It took me several weeks to make and install these panels. I was so engrossed with this project; I hardly heeded the social effects of the pandemic. The panels were of a sandwich construction consisting of a layer of reflective Mylar insulation, a layer of closed cell insulation, and a skin of dark brown vegan leather. I attached the panels to the hull using contact cement and made frames with rubbed bronze painted PVC soffit strips, that I attached with small stainless screws and finishing washers. If you can imagine a motorcycle's leather saddlebags, that is what the interior looks like. Having a thicker layer of insulation and Naugahyde fabric, the walls are soft and forgiving if you are slammed against them during a storm. They are also very comfortable while leaning against them. My reading nook is a place in the boat in the berth where the hull comes to a V. It's the perfect place to relax.

Condensation Tips

To avoid condensation around the portholes (windows) in the winter, I insulated them with bubble wrap and foam tape that you can find in the hardware section. The foam tape comes in a lot of different types and sizes and can sometimes be reused after being taken down and stored for the summer. The ones I use frequently are the D-shaped white vinyl and the wide flat gray ones used between a pickup bed and a camper shell. Although my boat is well sealed against drafts, there is enough forced ventilation to keep the interior from getting too humid. Mold can be a problem in boats with not enough airflow. I cut a hole in the deck over the toilet and installed a solar powered fan. This quiet fan runs constantly to exhaust odors, while a vent above the propane stove allows fresh air to come in. This provides enough air circulation that I rarely find any mold in the boat. The insulation not only keeps the boat warm in the winter and cool in the summer, but also prevents much of the outside noise from coming in. However, you can still hear wavelets splashing against the hull and the sound of raindrops on the deck.

Lessons Learned

Use only stainless steel, bronze, or aluminum fasteners and metal parts on your boat. Plain and galvanized steel will begin to rust as soon as you install it. Always use marine grade tin coated wire and heat shrink terminals for your electrical projects. With certain applications and for appliances like fans, well insulated wiring with heat shrinking terminals can be used, but only when not exposed to weather or water. Wood doesn't do well on boats. There are boats with beautiful extensive teak trim and decks, but I always hear the owner complain about how much upkeep they require. I replaced the rub rail around the entire boat with PVC soffit boards, and the grab rails/luggage rack with PVC pipe. These were as strong or stronger than the original teak trim and will last a good long time.

Required Safety Items for Your Boat

Now that I was done with the remodel, I remounted the safety equipment, including 2 fire extinguishers, and 3 combination smoke/carbon dioxide detectors. I exceeded the minimum requirements for safety equipment. I thought about things that might happen on the water and found easy to reach places to store enough life jackets for me and my guests. Skippers are responsible for the safety of their passengers. There are several very good marine safety web sites. Here is one that offers a list of equipment and rules mandated for the state of Washington: https://parks.wa.gov/about/rules-and-safety/ boater-education-safety/boating-equipment. You must also adhere to the U.S. Coast Guard safety rules. In addition, you will also need placards for your boat's Coast Guard inspection. One of them says to not throw garbage into the water. If your boat is of a certain size, you need to have a formal plan for disposing of your garbage. The other 2 rules are "don't spill your fuel into the water" and "don't pump your sewage into the water". You can find these placards at marine stores or on the Internet.

CHAPTER 15:
DINGHIES VS KAYAKS

I enjoy the physical work of mundane projects. It allows me time to ruminate on future steps. From time to time, I pondered on how best to reach shore from an anchorage. Inflatable dinghies are commonly mounted on larger motor or sail boats, with davits to secure them. I've seen inflatable dinghies being towed by smaller sailboats. But because inflatable boats are not very hydrodynamic, even though some of them come with hard floors and oarlocks, they need an outboard motor to push them around. Although the rubberized dinghies come with oars, I wouldn't have the strength to row them fast enough to get anywhere, especially against the tide. Although electric outboard motor prices are coming down, they can still be pricey. There are small, inexpensive 4 stroke gasoline motors, but since I wanted to use renewable energy as much as possible, I rejected using fossil fuel propulsion. Besides, it would be nearly impossible for me to lift a heavy dinghy and its motor over the side of a boat. Not to mention how hard it would be to bring the dinghy back into the boat when needed. I have seen some sailboats with their dinghy mounted on the forward deck by the bow. Smaller cabin cruisers generally mount their dinghy off the stern, while larger, more luxurious cruisers have theirs mounted above the main deck and employ a crane to drop the dinghy over the side. I could possibly mount a dinghy off the stern, but I already have enough stuff there, including the BBQ, ladder, crab trap, and the trolling motor. A rubberized or vinyl dinghy would have to be inflated and secured against the wind and waves. I wouldn't have time to manually inflate one under emergency conditions. It would have to be protected against the sun that would destroy the vinyl fabric. If I were to carry it on the fore deck, it also might catch the lines and interfere with the jib sail when tacking. It would most definitely get in the way while anchoring and mooring. On the plus side, they would be relatively safe to enter and exit from the sailboat and could carry an ice chest full of supplies.

Then I thought about kayaks. I have paddled many times since moving to Washington; With all its streams and lakes, not to mention Puget Sound, it is a kayaker's paradise. The long, sit-inside kayaks are better for ocean journeys, but I liked the idea of the sit-on-top kind. They're short so they fit well on the deck of my sailboat, unsinkable, and don't fill up with water if you capsize them. You could take the ones with a square stern to the beach and ride the waves. A kayak would be harder to enter and more likely to flip over than a dinghy. In the summer, falling in the water wouldn't be a problem. I'm a good swimmer, and always wear an inflatable life jacket. In the winter, I could wear the wetsuit I bought for inspecting the hull, prop, and for changing the zinc anodes. I decided that a kayak would be ideal for going ashore to register for a mooring ball or exploring islands or the state parks. I could buy a second kayak and mount my ice chest on it to safely carry groceries back to the boat when necessary. Kayaks could lay neatly in the scuppers and be secured with quick release knots so I could untie one quickly during an emergency. You get a good workout, and kayaking is fun! I also explored thoughts of how much fun it would be to have an electric powered kayak. I saw advertisements for already designed and built electric powered kayaks, but at the time, they started at $1200. I figured I could make my own custom kayak more cheaply. I started shopping around and found a Daylite sit-on-top kayak for $100 on Craigslist, an inexpensive electric trolling motor, and a small 12v battery for much less than I would spend on a dinghy or pre-built electric kayak. Daylite kayaks also only weigh 37 lbs. This one, being yellow, would be easily seen on the water. It wasn't designed to have a motor, but it had a squared off stern. I drove my van to the address and picked it up. Next stop, a marine store where I bought the 30 lb. thrust 12-volt electric trolling motor and the smallest 12v AGM battery I could find. Then I went to the hardware store and bought an 8-foot 1"x8" PVC soffit board for the motor mount. In the space of an afternoon, the project was finished. I waited until the next day for the 3M 5200 sealant to cure to take it for a test drive. The total weight of the kayak, motor and battery is about 70 lbs. I used the small block and tackle traveler attached to the mainsail boom on my boat to swing the kayak out into the water. Then I pulled the kayak around to the stern and let down the folding ladder. It was a little scary the first time getting into the kayak. I held onto the rail and supported most of my weight, gingerly placing a foot on either side of the front of the kayak, then dropped into the seat. Then I unhooked the kayak from the traveler and pushed off. One of my neighbors saw my modified kayak and me on our maiden voyage. "You're nuts", he said, "What will you dream up next?". I have a reputation with my liveaboard neighbors. Later, after repeating the process of entering the kayak a few times, it felt natural and comfortable. I would spend many hours enjoying driving and paddling this little kayak around. I weigh 180 lbs. and with the weight of the motor and battery, I was approaching the 250 lb. safe weight limit for the kayak. Next season I will mount a couple of small fenders to the sides near the stern for more flotation and stability. The fenders have holes where you normally tie the ropes to but would work perfectly for a sturdy 3/4" PVC pipe frame!

This is a good place to insert another disclaimer. I am not a marine engineer and am not recommending altering a consumer item. If you do this, you may endanger your own safety, and most likely are voiding the manufacturer's warranty. I am only relating my experience and am not liable for injury because of anything you do!

I ended up buying another new Daylite kayak on clearance for

$130. I would secure an ice chest to it and tow this kayak from my electric powered one. As a benefit, I would have an extra kayak for guests who want to go paddling! The kayaks are sitting in the gunnels on either side of my boat. At 37 pounds, they're light enough that I can pick them up with one hand and move them easily as needed.

CHAPTER 16:
PUGET SOUND

I was blessed to end up in the Pacific Northwest for a new job as an information technology contractor at Costco, a big box retailer headquartered in Issaquah, Washington. I was also blessed with a colleague who liked to sail with members of her yacht club. There are several large lakes in and around Seattle, and they flow into Puget Sound, a vast extent of navigable waters. According to Wikipedia, Puget Sound is part of the Salish Sea, which also includes the bodies of water surrounding the San Juan Islands, the Straits of Georgia, and the Straits of Juan de Fuca. Puget Sound extends approximately 100 miles from Deception Pass in the north to Olympia in the south. Its average depth is 450 feet and its maximum depth, off Jefferson Point between Indianola and Kingston, is 930 feet. The depth of the main basin, between the southern tip of Whidbey Island and Tacoma, is approximately 600 feet. Puget Sound's shoreline is 1,332 miles long, encompassing a water area of 1,020 square miles. I found out from reading the Wikipedia entry that it has total volume of 26.5 cubic miles at mean high water, and the average volume of water flowing in and out of Puget Sound during each tide is 1.26 cubic miles. Although I haven't made the passage through Deception pass, I found that tidal currents there are in the range of 9 to 10 knots. That's fast. Most mariners I have talked to about Deception Pass will only transit it during slack tides, even with motorboats! The geological history of Puget Sound is also very interesting. Arnold, my first sailing instructor, told me and the crew about how the glaciers from the last ice age spread and retreated several times, scouring and depressing the land, then melting to leave what we see now. He would point out the soft clay and sand cliffs, many of which had houses built on top of them. He said clay was on the bottom layers, and the top layers were compressed sand. When the rain percolates through the sand, it causes the clay to get slippery, resulting in a landslide. I remembered that a landslide recently occurred just north of Seattle, wiping out an entire town!

Arnold also talked about the subduction zones and faults in the area. While there have been smaller earthquakes in the area, there have been major ones in the past. There are records of a major magnitude nine earthquake in the Cascadia subduction zone in the 1700's. I hope I am not anywhere near Seattle during the next major earthquake! Can you imagine the tidal wave during the big one? In the San Juan archipelago alone, there are over 400 islands and rocks, 128 of which are named. A former colleague of mine, a Geocacher, told me of old forts and buildings he has explored on some of these islands. I could spend the rest of my life sailing the Salish Sea and exploring the lands it borders.

CHAPTER 17: THE ADVENTURES BEGIN!

As I became more confident in my abilities while sailing around Commencement Bay outside of Tacoma, Washington, I wanted to start taking longer trips and explore farther reaches of the Sound. I also needed to learn how to anchor. My marina neighbors mentioned that Quartermaster Harbor, located between Vashon Island on the west and Maury Island on the east, across the bay from Tacoma, was a perfect place to spend the night. It was an easy afternoon trip across the bay from Tacoma and was an ideal place to practice anchoring. It was well out of the way from traffic zones, protected from bad weather by hills from all sides, and had a long, gently sloping mud bottom. Although I had used anchors with a small boat in freshwater lakes in the past, this would be my first time anchoring a large boat in the sea. So, I set off one afternoon across the bay to the harbor. Entering the harbor, I saw only two other small sailboats anchored in the shallow harbor. It wasn't crowded at all. This would be a good place to try out the Danforth anchor that came with the boat. This is a common type of anchor. The blades of this anchor can swing up at right angles in relationship to the shaft, so it has a good grip on many types of bottom surfaces. Although anchors for smaller boats can be tied directly to nylon rope, larger boats generally use chain or a combination of chain and nylon rope. The rope, chain, or rope and chain combination is termed the "rode". In the chain/nylon configuration, the chain is fastened to the anchor and the nylon rope is spliced to the chain. Chain is much more resistant to abrasion from rocks, and nylon rope is used because it stretches and provides protection against the shock that waves can produce. The chain provides additional holding power because it will lay along the bottom and helps keep the anchor from being pulled straight up. There are a lot of anchoring articles available on the Internet. Some are very technical and use mathematical formulas. Other articles are simple "rule of thumb" guides from experienced sailors. I don't understand why, but most of these articles don't mention the state of the tide, whether it is high or low when measuring the depth. When anchoring at sea, I generally use 30 feet plus 4 times the water depth at low tide. There are many variables that need to be considered while anchoring, including the positions of other boats anchored near you, the composition of the bottom, whether sand, rock, or mud, the slope of the bottom, and how close you are to the shore. I may anchor in deeper water if the bottom rises sharply or lay more rode out if a storm is expected. After the anchor is out and with the rode secured on the cleat, I reverse the boat with the current to set the anchor. I have used this method for 2 seasons, in all kinds of weather, wind and waves, and my boat hasn't drifted off yet. Sailboats usually come with 2 anchors, one fore and one aft. The sailboats I have seen anchored in Puget Sound have always had only the bow anchor out. The boats will swing around with the tides, and to a lesser extent, the wind. It makes sense to set the bow anchor out for the current and waves to have less force on the boat and therefore have less chance of pulling the anchor out. To avoid hitting other boats, make sure you have the same number of anchors and the same length of rode out as the other boats near you. You can tell by the angle of the anchor line from other boats to estimate how much line they have out. The more rope you have out will obviously increase the circumference your boat will circle in as the tide changes. As a point of etiquette, when I'm anchoring among other boats, I ask my neighbors if they have any issues with me mooring near them. Some boats have an electric windlass, which gives a mechanical advantage when it comes time to pull the anchor up when it's time to go. My boat doesn't have one. When a boat is anchored for several days, the anchor can dig into the mud on the bottom, making it difficult to pull up. I remembered a technique I read about years earlier. You could drive your boat forward against the current to pull the stubborn anchor out of the mud, making it much easier to lift out of the water. Some other things to consider are turning on your all-around light when you are anchored at night, especially in places not usually used for anchoring, and keeping out of boat travel routes. Most bodies of water have regulations on where to anchor, and how long you can stay in one place. Read up on that to stay out of trouble. Here is a link for Washington State anchoring laws: https://apps.leg.wa.gov/wac/default.aspx?cite=332-52-155. Finally, if you are in an area with homes on the shore, be considerate. In other words, don't be that person that gives sailors a bad name!

My First Week-long Trip

For a sailor, "adventure" sometimes means something went terribly wrong. Sailors who successfully managed their way out of trouble and survived, are accordingly granted story telling rights. My yacht club encourages its members to tell such tales at the meetings. These tales can serve as cautionary lessons meant to warn new sailors of dangers and conditions inherent while sailing in various locations around Puget Sound.

Such is this story of my first crossing under the Tacoma Narrows bridge. Although the prudent sailor plans out the trip from one point to the next, considers the weather and tides, studies marine charts, reads the travel guides, and ensures all critical systems are good to go, bad things can happen.

I started planning a week-long off the grid trip to the south Puget Sound area. I had heard from a friend about a popular boating destination, Cutts Island, which is near Kopachuck State Park. He told me it was a nice place to go, and there were several mooring balls around the island. Mooring balls are small buoys anchored firmly to the bottom with steel rings on top that are used to tie boats up to. So, I stocked up on provisions for a week and charted out the journey. I would leave my marina in Tacoma, go north around Point Defiance, south under the Tacoma Narrows Bridge, then spend a week in the Kopachuck and Penrose Point State Park areas. These state marine parks also had mooring balls. Since I bought the Washington State Parks unlimited moorage permit, I wanted to take advantage of it and check out as many state parks as possible. Here is a link for Washington State Parks where you can purchase the permit: https://parks.wa.gov/passes-permits/permits/moorage-permit.

Crossing Under the Tacoma Narrows Bridge

Do you remember the old black-and-white film in your science or physics class of the wildly swaying bridge that shook itself to pieces over a canyon? That was the original Tacoma Narrows bridge, nicknamed "Galloping Gerty". According to news reports, it was completed on July 1, 1940. A few months later, on November 7, 1940, it was filmed during a period of moderate wind. Apparently, the engineers didn't consider the harmonic vibrations that would occur when the wind blew at a certain speed. Kind of like how blowing on a reed between your lips makes it vibrate and produce a sound. This harmonic vibration caused the bridge to sway with increasing violence until it shook itself apart. Engineers learned a lot from this failure, and later a new bridge was built in its place. The old bridge on the bottom of the Narrows was once the third longest suspension bridge in the world. Now it is said to hold the world record for the largest man-made reef. The Tacoma Narrows Bridge is on State Highway 16 and is the major land route that connects Tacoma to Gig Harbor and separates the North Puget Sound from South Puget Sound. The steep topography of the canyon walls extends under water. Because there are large bodies of water on either side of the bridge, the tidal currents occurring during peak ebb and flood tides can become very strong, fast, and unpredictable. I always read the sailor's guidebook before each trip. The book tells me that "the current floods on the east side and ebbs on the west side, most of the time (but not all of the time)". Such were the conditions when I attempted my first crossing under the Tacoma Narrows Bridge. When planning for the trip, I timed the segments of the journey to take advantage of the tide going out until I reached Point Defiance, then the incoming tide would help push me through the Tacoma Narrows. On the day of the trip, a fresh breeze was coming against me from the north. To save time, I had to motor to the point. Then, I had to wait 20 minutes to let the Tacoma to Vashon Island ferry pass before continuing. There are 3 marine passages around Point Defiance. They are the Colvos, the Delco, and the Narrows. As I reached that area, it was interesting to watch the interplay of the currents in the water. The water was churning with sediment, seafoam, and debris including tree branches and lumber washed in from land by rivers. This five-mile leg of the trip took longer than I anticipated, but then I was around the point and heading south. I put the sails up to get some extra speed and made up some time approaching the Narrows. I had entered during flood tide, and things were going well. Just after I passed under the bridge, unfortunately, the tide changed and started ebbing out. At the same time, the wind, which had been blowing from the north suddenly started blowing strongly from the south. My boat spun around, and the jib sheet line wrapped itself around the starboard spreader and tore it off. Luckily, the spreader was still attached to the shroud supporting the mast. The jib sail was now useless, and it was getting dark; the sun was setting. I dropped the mainsail and motored around Point Fosdick to starboard into Hale Passage. I had used a lot of battery power while cruising around towards Point Defiance, so I limped around all night on the trolling motor to avoid using up my main batteries. While I used the trolling motor for fishing, and as a side-thruster to get into tight mooring spaces, this was my "plan C" if something were to go wrong with my main inboard drive motor and I couldn't sail. The friend who had told me about Cutts Island State Park said I might be able to get there by going under the Fox Island Bridge. When I researched the Fox Island Bridge before the trip, I was unable to find how tall it was; even though everything else about the bridge and the history of Fox Island was published in a Wikipedia entry. If the bridge was tall enough for the mast to fit under, it would save me from having to sail miles around Fox Island to get to Cutts Island. It was a beautiful, warm summer night. The wind had died down, the sky was clear, the stars were bright, and a full moon rose over the horizon. Around 1 AM, I got close enough to the bridge to see it. Almost too close, the imposing mass loomed above me. But it wasn't tall enough for my boat's mast to pass underneath it. I reversed the boat and headed slowly east and back to the main channel. While I was making my way down Hale Passage and around Fox Island in the dark, I kept hearing a strange noise like someone taking deep breaths before diving in a swimming pool. This sound continued off and on for several hours. As dawn broke, the morning light revealed to me the culprit. A sea lion had accompanied me all the way from the Fox Island bridge to the Narrows channel. I swear he winked at me and shook his head as he dove under the water and left me. Ever since then I have had an affinity for sea lions. They often accompany me on my trips. While I have observed seals at rest on docks, they haven't exhibited the same friendliness. You can tell the difference between sea lions and seals by the shape of their muzzle and ears. Sea lions have ear flaps and squared-off muzzles, whereas seals' muzzles are slender and pointed, with only holes on the side of their heads where their ears are. After many sailing trips, I encountered some of the transient Orcas feeding on a seal or sea lion carcass, and I wondered if sea lions swim near my boat to hide from these killer whales! Crossing under the Narrows bridge was a harrowing experience. I believe there should be a t-shirt or ceremony for that rite of passage, like they have for crossing the equator...

Cutts Island

After leaving Hale Passage, just south of the Narrows Bridge, I felt a gentle wind blowing from the southeast. It would probably be OK to hoist the sails, even with the broken spreader. Although one of the stays was slack because of the broken spreader, there were five others to hold the mast in position. I hoisted up the main sail and jib, and we glided around Fox Island towards Kopachuck State Park and Cutts Island. Then the wind swung around from the south and steadily grew stronger. Cutts Island came into view. The island is small, maybe an acre or two in area. The south rises almost cliff-like from the water, whereas the north end slopes gently to a long, sandy beach. As I drew closer, I could see sea lions strewn along the shallow beach and hear them barking and arguing with each other. You probably know those sounds. The wind was getting stronger as I dropped the sails and glided towards a mooring ball. After tying up to the mooring ball and packing the sails away, I went down to fix supper. The waves started to get higher, maybe 3 or 4 feet high, and I was starting to feel seasick. I had bought meclizine seasickness tablets, just in case, but hoping to never use them. It's funny, even after spending years on boats, I still get seasick. I took the tablets and felt better.

Tips on Using a Mooring Ball

Washington State Parks limit the size of boats tying up to the mooring balls to 45'. If your boat is bigger than that, you will have to look for an anchorage in the area. After you reach your destination, either at a state park mooring ball or a protected harbor where you would like to spend a few days, here are some things to know and keep in mind. Washington state law allows you to stay at a state mooring ball for up to 3 nights. In 2023, it costs $15 per night, and you were required to either register at the drop box on shore or by phone. Phone registration costs an additional $4.50. When I first used the phone to register, the person who answered the phone didn't know where Blake Island was. Which made me suspect that these calls were going to a privately operated generic call center not in the state of Washington. I assume the registration was required for occupancy statistics around the various state parks, but to me it felt inefficient. I'm sure there are many companies in the Seattle area who would love to create an online app for registering at state parks. Having this data available immediately would be beneficial for Washington State Parks staffing, maintenance, and fee enforcement.

I sail single-handed most of the time when camping on my boat. After a few experiences, I learned an easy and practical way of tying up. I keep the 25-foot bow lines loosely tied on the stanchions close to the cockpit within easy reach. I approach the mooring ball against the tide. The mooring ball, made of a tough plastic, would gently rub and bump on the hull as it came closer to the cockpit. As soon as I could reach the steel ring set into the top of the ball, I would pass the end of the bowline through the ring and temporarily tie the line around the jib sail line cleat. I then put the boat into neutral, letting the boat drift slowly backwards so the mooring ball would slide up towards the bow. Then I would take the bowline off the cleat and walk it forward. I would then tie it off to the anchor cleat, while leaving some slack. The bow lines have a rubber snubber that takes the shock from waves away from the line. I also have a short 10-foot mooring line looped through the anchor guide wheel support, which is a heavy-duty stainless-steel bar that flexes a little as it hangs over the bow. I would pass this line through the mooring ball's ring, then tie it off to the anchor cleat. This gives me peace of mind that if one line broke or came untied, I had a second rope holding my boat secure. My boat would not drift off in the middle of the night into the path of a cargo ship or be grounded on shore. With two lines securing the mooring ball in this way also keeps the mooring ball from bumping into the side of your boat, something that kept me from sleeping well at night. You should also leave some extra slack in your lines according to the state of the tides. One day, I tied my boat very closely to a mooring ball during low tide. After a few hours, I had a weird premonition, so I checked the lines again. The bow of the boat was being pulled down as the tide rose, as if attached to a giant sinker. There is a possibility that a boat could be swamped with water and sink if tied off too tightly!

When you're boating, it's good practice to pull up the fenders. Some captains even stow the fenders away, instead of leaving them in the gunnels so they don't impede the crew. It also looks better from the viewpoint of other boats as leaving the fenders out is a sign of inexperienced boaters. Handling the fenders like this is time consuming and one more thing to remember to do before docking the boat. I made this easier by tying ropes to the bottom of my fenders on each side and leading the lines back to the cockpit where I could reach them. This way, I can pull the fenders up when sailing, and put them back down easily before docking.

Repairing the Spreader

After I tied up to a mooring ball at Cutts Island, I proceeded to check out the damage to the spreader. Fortunately, one of my earlier projects was to install steps going up the mast. They were a 2-part step made of some kind of fiber reinforced ultraviolet-light resistant plastic. The inside part of the step was attached to the mast with rivets, and the step part could be folded up out of the way when no longer needed. I use a mountain climbing harness when I must spend time up the mast. I used rock climbing gear while mountain climbing as a teenager. I was comfortable using it and wouldn't go up a mast without it. The general idea for its use is to avoid falling. I would use two Prusik knots, which are loops of rope wrapped around the shrouds and attached to a carabiner on the harness, to keep from falling all the way to the deck if I were to lose my balance. Prusik knots will tighten when pulling on the long loop, and slide by pushing up on the part looped around the shroud. I was therefore able to safely climb up the mast and examine the spreader. The spreaders were mounted to a bracket attached to a fastener that was bolted through the mast. The mounting bracket had been ripped by the stress of the strong wind on the sail. Fortunately, the other end of the spreader was clipped to the shroud, otherwise it would have been lost if it had fallen overboard. I unbolted the damaged bracket and took it down into the cockpit. I had kept all my tools on the boat, including a battery-operated metal cutting saw, a drill, some clamps, and tools to bend metal with. I also had a stout sheet of aluminum from a discarded stop sign that I found in the trash. It occurred to me that somewhere, an intersection might be missing a stop sign. I hoped not! It was starting to get dark, and I was weary from not sleeping the previous night. I cooked supper on the grill, watched the sunset, and slept like a log. The next day, as I made the new bracket, the south wind steadily increased. While climbing the mast to install the new bracket for the spreader, I saw another sailboat approach and tie up to another mooring ball. It was difficult to reattach the spreader because the waves were growing stronger and making the mast sway. I finished the job, tightened the turnbuckle on the shroud, and went back down into the cabin. I was proud of myself for getting out of my first bad situation! The next day I noticed the other sailboat was gone. They apparently decided it would be better to ride the windstorm out somewhere else. When mooring and expecting a storm, consider which direction the cove or inlet is facing. If your boat is exposed, you will feel the full, uncomfortable effect of the wind pushing the waves toward you. I found out later that the north side of Cutts Island had a gradually sloping sandy bottom. It would have been much better to anchor there.

The next morning was Saturday. Soon after I brewed coffee and had eaten breakfast, all manner of boats swarmed the area. There were cabin cruisers, small motorboats including wakeboard boats, and jet skis. Some of the boats landed on the beach and the sea lions took to the water. One of the motorboats came up to me and I saw a familiar face. It was a member of the crew who sailed my neighbor's boat at the Foss Harbor Marina! After the Wednesday evening sailboat races, she and her friends would stop and chat with me occasionally. They even gave me desserts or wine left over from their picnics after the races. She introduced her family on their little boat. We spoke for a few minutes, then they made their way to the beach. My friend at Foss Harbor Marina was right about this island being popular on the weekends!

Powerboats Driving Through Designated Swimming Areas

I usually attend Seattle's yearly springtime boat show. Mostly to get free swag, and drool over brand new Beneteau sailboats that I may never be able to afford. There are all kinds of boats there, from jet skis to rowboats and cabin cruisers. Over the years, I have noticed a trend towards fast little boats that are purposely designed to throw up huge wakes for water boarders and jet skiers to jump over.

I watched, horrified, as these wakeboard boats and jet skis cut through the swimming area that was cordoned off with buoys that were clearly marked with "SWIMMING AREA, DO NOT ENTER". I don't know why wakeboard boats are even allowed on Puget Sound. It's not just the noise, which interferes with water mammals hunting, but their wake erodes the shoreline! These little boats are going so fast that sea mammals don't have any time to dive and avoid being injured by propellers. It's no surprise that the group of Southern Resident Orcas who make Puget Sound their home are starving and dying. While I was at the boat show, there was a booth giving out free "Whale Sighted" flags. I keep mine handy in case I see any whales. I have a mind to start flying it whenever I see seals or sea lions!

Anyway, people were starting to drink and party and turning their music up loud. Nobody else seemed to mind, though, so I left Cutts Island and freed up a mooring ball for someone else. One good thing about boating is, if you don't like your neighborhood, you can always go somewhere else!

My First Invitation to Go Ashore for a Meal

After leaving Cutts Island, I wanted to stop at Penrose Point State Park to explore the area, get some supplies, and see Lakebay Marina. Lakebay Marina is in Mayo Cove on Key Peninsula, around the corner from Penrose Point State Park. I had read an article about Lakebay Marina closing. https://www.dnr.wa.gov/programs-and-services/aquatics/aquatic-lands-restoration-team/lakebay-marina-redevelopment. The Washington State Department of Natural Resources bought it and is planning to renovate it. I wanted to see it before work started. I got a late start casting off the mooring ball at Cutts Island. After a blissful, relaxing afternoon of sailing, I neared Penrose Point State Park. I sailed up and down the shoreline for a while but couldn't identify either the state park or Lakebay Marina, even with binoculars. Later, when discussing Penrose State Park with some neighbors, they told me that the marina and state park were hard to find. One would have to venture into the shallow cove to see them. It was getting dark when I saw some mooring balls. I assumed they were for the state park, so I let the sails down and quietly motored to the nearest one and started tying up, when I heard someone on the shore yell, "Are you all right?". I acknowledged that I was, then doubt struck me. "Is this Penrose State Park?", I yelled back. "No", he said. "This is a private moorage, but you're welcome to stay here overnight". "The state park is the next point over", he said. I gratefully accepted his hospitality, cooked for the evening, and retired. The next morning, I made coffee and was cooking breakfast on the grill, when I saw my host climbing down the stairs from his house; "Would you like to come ashore for coffee?", he asked. I thanked him, while holding up my cup. "Would you like breakfast?", he asked. I looked at my kayak and decided it would be too much trouble to go ashore, and politely turned down his request. In retrospect, I should have accepted his invitation. I just wasn't used to people being so friendly that they would invite me, a stranger, to breakfast. This would be the first of many invitations I received to join people and share meals and stories while on my journey. While anchoring, I thought I would get complaints from people on the shore; I would spoil their view. But it turns out that people like to meet others who grab the rope in their teeth and set off on adventures!

Post-pandemic Summer Events

I spent the rest of the summer taking SSYC yacht club members out on sailing trips, having barbecues with my neighbors, and enjoying retirement and the relaxing boating life. One day, I invited a neighbor at the marina to sail with me. He and his wife had their own racing/cruising sailboat and lived in it. They both travelled a lot for business and didn't get many chances to sail together. They made a pact, although they were both very good sailors, they wouldn't take the boat out without both present. Losing or damaging the boat would be unforgiveable. One weekend, while the wife was away, I invited the husband for a day sail. He was a very good sailor and skippered a racing crew on a boat in Portland, Oregon. It was a good day for sailing with a steady brisk wind from the east. We got my boat up over 9 knots that afternoon; the fastest my boat had even been since I owned it. I received a great adrenaline rush as we sailed on a beam reach to the wind, the scuppers close to the surface of the water, but never going under. I felt safe with this experienced racer next to me. I handled the tiller and jib, while he sat on the edge of the cockpit and managed the mainsail. I learned a lot about balancing the sails while having this experienced sailor with me. I recommend you take every advantage of sailing with a racing crew member.

In the fall, I attended a friend's Halloween party. I dressed up as a clump of seaweed. Everyone liked dancing with me, and I won first prize in the men's costume contest! By the winter of 2022, most of the boat projects were done. I thought about my career and considered going back to work. During the pandemic, there was no gradual weaning off work pressures towards retirement for me. One day I had a fulfilling career, meetings, stress and a thousand demands on my time, on the next, nothing. I'm glad I had the boat to work on after being laid off. But the work on the boat was done, and now I was bored. Some of our yacht club members participated in a winter race series on Lake Union called the "Goosebumps" series. In the past I would help crew the sailboats in the race, but not this year. It was too far to drive. So, I read, studied, and plotted my summer journey around the Puget Sound Area. And I went to the occasional yacht club happy hour or dance.

The Flamingo Dance

My yacht club hosts monthly dances during the year, sometimes with a DJ and sometimes with a live band. The theme at one of the spring dances was the "Flamingo Dance". The theme was that the ladies would wear pink, and the gentlemen would wear suits with a pink tie. Curiosity got the better of me, so I googled how flamingos danced so I could learn it and demonstrate it at the occasion. You must check it out on YouTube. It's cute. The girl flamingos would gather on one side of the beach, while the boy flamingos lined up in rows on the other end. The dance was a ritual in which the girl flamingos would select their lifelong mate. The dance was simple. The boys tucked their wings up next to their body and stood up very straight. Then they would all step side by side quickly in unison to their left, stand, swivel their heads quickly left, right, left. Then they would all shuffle to the right and swivel their heads again. The male flamingos would repeat the dance until they were all taken out of the lineup. Darned if I could tell one flamingo from another!

The Daffodil Parade

The Tacoma Yacht Club hosts an annual "Daffodil Parade". This happens on the 2nd weekend in April and runs from Friday through Sunday. The Tacoma Yacht Club has a large, modern facility suitable for hundreds of guests. There are a lot of fun activities, including a trivia contest with teams of representatives from the attending yacht clubs, meals served by caterers, dances and finally on Sunday, the Daffodil Parade. The parade features boats decorated with a daffodil flower theme. 1000's of the bright yellow early emerging flowers are consumed for this event! Although my own boat wasn't in the parade, I took a marina slip for the weekend and attended the festivities. It was nice to go down to my boat after dancing all night and sleep in the berth instead of having to drive home. This event was a pleasant prelude to Opening Day!

Opening Day - Festivities on Lake Union

Seattle's Opening Day, which marks the official start of boating season in the area, occurs over the first weekend in May. This would be my first Opening Day experience. In previous years, I was either working or on-call and never had a chance to attend this event. Opening Day was hosted by Seattle Yacht Club. They have this link for the schedules: https://seattleyachtclub.org/opening-day. Among the many activities and events scheduled were a dock walk where boaters host food and drinks on their boats and walk up and down the dock while visiting with sailors from other yacht clubs. This year we were honored to have boats and crew from the Canadian Navy Auxiliary at the end of the dock. There was even a "border" you had to stop at and correctly answer trivia questions before proceeding to the "Canadian" side of the dock. In the evenings, the captains and crew would don their uniforms, blue blazers with white trousers or skirts for the formal dinners and dances. On Saturday, there is a boat parade. Boats in the parade are decorated and compete in contests with various categories. There were categories for both power and sail boats. One of them was "Best Classic Motorboat". While wandering around, I encountered some beautiful old boats with their polished wood and brass. A panel of judges selects winners of each category, who will receive a small trophy and have their boat and club names engraved on a plaque and added to a much larger trophy residing at Seattle Yacht Club. Members of my club, the Seattle Singles Yacht Club, have entered the "Best Decorated Sailboat" for many years. This year, 2023, would be no exception. The Seattle Yacht Club provided a theme for the decorations. This year it was "board games", in which entrants would dream up a game like "Operation" or "Chutes and Ladders" and attempt to model it in human size on their boats. One of our club's members entered this contest, and several members of the club and I volunteered to help decorate their boat. Our boat's theme was the game "Mousetrap". That is the game consisting of a course, somewhat like mini-golf, or a "Rube Goldberg" device, where a steel ball rolling down a ramp would follow the course. Its last action was to set off a trigger and drop a cage over a plastic mouse. Over several weekends and nights, we built a life-size model of the game.

Since I was good with tools and making stuff, I was tasked with building props and parts out of plywood. The artists in our team stayed true to the colors on the game board and painted the parts. On the weekend before Opening Day, we did a dry fit of the pieces before attaching them to the boat. This activity reminded me of my high school days when making floats for school parades. The group had a lot of fun and we took this opportunity to deepen our friendships. During the construction, the sailboat's owner and skipper asked me to help pilot the boat from her marina in south Seattle through the locks to Lake Union and to Dock Zero of the Seattle Yacht Club. I would earn the benefit of having a close place to stay over the 3-day festivities. Our team met on Dock Zero to assemble and attach the mousetrap to the boat. At the same time, we took breaks and participated in the festivities on the dock. Assembling the Mousetrap game on the sailboat was a little challenging, but at the end of the day, it looked good and sturdy. The next day was parade day. We woke up, had a quick breakfast, and completed the finishing touches on the decorated boat. Unfortunately, we somehow missed the starting bell, and were a few minutes late in joining the parade. Our skipper fretted about this while slaloming through the anchored boats to our position in the parade. She was worried that we would lose points for being late. In the end, the rest of the boats were behind schedule, too, so our tardiness wasn't noticeable. As we cruised along the parade route, many of the spectators waved and called out from their boats.

We got back to Dock Zero, and in the afternoon, attended the awards ceremony. We had won first place in the decorated sailboat category! When our boat was called out, the crew and several other members of our club climbed onstage to accept our trophy. I looked over at our skipper. She was so overcome with emotion; I saw a tear rolling down her cheek! Later, after the presentation was complete, I walked back up to the stage where all the big trophies for the contest categories were. While looking at the rows of the winners' engraved names, I noticed our club had won the "Best Decorated Sailboat" prize many times over the years. It felt good to win again for our club!

CHAPTER 18: THE 2ND TIME AROUND

During the winter of 2022, I decided to liquidate the household furniture and belongings I had kept in storage. Along with my slip at Foss Harbor Marina, I had rented a combination storage unit/workshop. It was very handy, just a short walk from my boat. I was comfortable enough in my tiny sailboat house and was confident enough in my boat life that I wasn't going to move back to land anytime soon. At night I placed advertisements on Craigslist, and during the day I would take calls and move the stuff out of my storage unit. Over the winter I had planned my summer trips. If everything went well, I could explore the San Juan Islands for a whole summer.

Delays

My boat was ready to go for the 2023 sailing season. The weather was getting warmer, the days were getting longer, and it had finally stopped raining here in the Seattle area. Residents were looking forward to the long sunny days and warm, dry summers that came with the Pacific Northwest climate. After having remodeled my boat while living aboard here at Foss Harbor Marina, I was finally ready to cast off and head north to the San Juan Islands. I would meet some of my liveaboard friends and neighbors who had been planning their own trips to various exotic locations after making a shakedown cruise to Soucie Island in the San Juan Island archipelago north of Seattle. I planned to leave on my trip on June 1, 2023. Unfortunately, before I was ready to leave, my car was vandalized for the 5th time while parked in the marina parking lot. In the past the perps stole gas from my van, once by puncturing a hole in the bottom of the gas tank, and once by sticking a hose through the filler tube. They couldn't remove the hose, so they left it there. One morning, I came out to find one of my tires slashed. I had a full-sized spare, but I didn't have the special tool to release the tire from under the van, so I had to ride my bicycle to the auto parts store and get an extension for my socket wrench to lower the tire. I found out later that a neighbor's car had its catalytic converter stolen that same night. My car didn't have a catalytic converter. It had been stolen before I bought the van, and the previous owner had a straight pipe welded in place. I imagined that the perp had rolled under my van with its high clearance, thinking it would be easy pickings, and slashed the tire because there was no catalytic converter. Although I had installed a dash camera that recorded every break-in, that didn't seem to deter the crimes. I had a homemade motion detector, but I forgot to turn it on one night. My car was broken into that night and the perps stole the alarm, along with my gym bag. My neighbors had been reporting thefts and vandalism for months. People were having their car windows smashed, tires slashed, and catalytic converters stolen. Some cars and motorcycles had been stolen. Although the marina management had recently put in a gate to prevent unauthorized cars from entering the parking lot, it wasn't enough to keep anyone from walking in. These crimes were occurring with increasing frequency and severity of damage. This time someone tried to steal my entire car. The young man tried, unsuccessfully, to start it by turning the ignition switch with a pair of channel-lock pliers. He gave up trying to steal the van and started methodically removing my belongings from the car. He made trip after trip, removing my belongings and throwing them over the fenced-in parking lot, to pick them up later. He took my gym bag with workout clothing and toiletries, my jumpstart battery pack with air compressor, the propane heater I used on camping trips, and some tools. They always steal my gym bag. How do I know it was a young man who tried to steal my car? After the first time it was vandalized, I installed a dash cam that recorded the surroundings continuously. I had video of the people who spiked the bottom of the gas tank and captured a few gallons of fuel, while the remainder of the 20-gallon tank drained into the harbor. I found it costs $1000 to have a replacement, used gas tank installed. Fortunately, JB Weld makes gas tank repair epoxy glue for $9.99. The tank is still holding gas a year later! Anyway, if your car is vandalized in Tacoma, the police ask you to fill out an incident report on the internet. However, if the thieves try to steal the entire car, it is categorized differently. In these cases, the police will take video submissions attached to the incident. Anyway, the police department say they will increase patrols according to how much crime is in an area. I haven't seen a police car patrolling this area, even after people here at the marina have reported hundreds of incidents. I can only wonder how bad things are in other areas of Tacoma. I had a workshop/garage/storage unit at the marina. Since I had sold all my household goods and furniture, I decided to take some time to make a spot for my van where it would be out of sight and much more difficult to vandalize. I didn't want to be somewhere many days' journey from the marina and get a call from the staff telling me that my car had been vandalized again.

I gave my notice to the marina that I was vacating my slip. It was now the middle of June, and I could finally go! For the first leg of the trip, I sailed north from Tacoma through Colvos Passage to reach my first stop, Blake Island State Park. The Colvos Passage channel is noted for the tendency of the current to flow north, regardless of whether it was ebb (going out) or flood (coming in) tide. Normally the fee to tie up at a state park mooring ball is $15 per night but I had purchased the annual Washington State Parks mooring permit for $150.00. This allows unlimited mooring at state parks with some caveats: a 3-day limit at most parks and you are required to register either by phone or by going onshore to fill out a payment envelope. It costs $4.50 to register by phone, so I would usually take my kayak to shore to register.

Another Setback

It was getting dark as I pulled up to Blake Island State Park. I found a vacant mooring ball and started the tying up process. The tie up procedure was going along fine, but I underestimated the speed and strength of the current on the south side of Blake Island. I should have swung my boat around for another try, but I thought I was strong enough to hold the boat against the current. I was strong enough, but unfortunately, my bones must have gotten more brittle over the years. I cracked a rib against the side of the cockpit while straining to hold the boat. In an instant, my plan to travel to the San Juan Islands was terminated. Though the cracked rib wasn't that painful, I wouldn't want to risk another more serious injury by taking chances on the wilder water in the straits in the passage to the San Juans. I would have to postpone the trip to Soucie Island until next year and spend the rest of the summer resting and touring Puget Sound. In the end it wasn't so bad.

Bremerton Pre 4th Meetup

My sailing club, Seattle Singles Yacht Club (SSYC), planned a meetup at Port Orchard Marina for the pre-4th of July firework celebration in Bremerton. It's a little easier to get into Port Orchard than the Bremerton Marina because the current doesn't run as fast there. Our fleet captain had reserved some spots at the guest dock. I had driven to Bremerton's celebration the previous year to watch the fireworks with some former neighbors. They lived on the cliff right next to the bridge that the fireworks were being fired from, and we had a fantastic view. A new type of fireworks was set off, like a light shower. After the lights entered the water, they burst back out like a reverse waterfall. They were awesome! Anyway, a few weeks before this meetup to watch this year's fireworks, I had given my "Electric Repower project" presentation at the yacht club, and everybody wanted to tour my boat. One visitor was recovering from shoulder surgery and although the stitches had healed, her arm was still in a sling. She toured the boat and was ready to disembark. I volunteered to assist her by supporting her arm on the good side and standing to the left of her. My boat is stable, and it doesn't move when you step on or off it, so I didn't expect anything to go wrong. Unfortunately, as she stepped out, she tripped over the rub rail. Although I was strong enough due to the physical nature of sailing, I wasn't prepared for or expecting to carry her entire weight. I did for a few seconds, but then the hamstring on my left leg tore and gave out. The spectators said it was like watching a train crash in slow motion. The lady was fine, thankfully, because she landed on me. Unfortunately, not only did I pull my hamstring, but I aggravated an old motorcycle injury to my knee and tore my posterior cruciate ligament. I could barely walk and couldn't join the rest of the group as they cast their boats off and motored to the middle of the harbor to watch the fireworks. I took an ice pack from my first-aid kit and an ibuprofen and watched some of the fireworks. I had to use binoculars to see them. I stayed an extra day at Port Orchard and increased circulation to my injury by slowly walking around the tourist area downtown. I had a good-sized bruise on my thigh and swelling behind my knee. One of the things I miss while sailing to remote areas and being on the water for days was ice cream, so I took this opportunity to indulge in a waffle cone. As I enjoyed the ice cream, while basking in the warm sun, my thoughts kept returning to the accident on my boat. It could have had a much worse outcome. My friend's injury could have been aggravated or we could have had ended up in the water. I committed myself to engineer a compact ramp with a handrail to make it easier to come aboard my boat. Did I mention that you should keep liability insurance for you and your boat?

Reciprocal Moorage

One of the best benefits from belonging to a yacht club is

reciprocal moorage. This is free or low-cost moorage offered by a yacht club to members from other yacht clubs. This courtesy is meant to foster networking and socialization among the sailing community, while providing sailors with more moorage options. I have used this benefit several times on my trips and have met many fine people! The club I belong to, Seattle Singles Yacht Club has over 100 reciprocal agreements with yacht clubs in Washington, Oregon, and British Columbia, Canada. They come with some caveats and restrictions, including length of stay per visit, the number of visits per year, and incidental fees. There is a website called yachtdestinations.org that displays details of the reciprocal moorage available for each yacht club. I found the information on the website was updated regularly and accurate, but you should always call your prospective yacht club ahead of time to confirm availability.

Bremerton to Eagle Harbor

I started planning my next passage. I had been to Eagle Harbor several times, but not with my own boat. One of my yacht club's favorite raft-up locations was Eagle Harbor, but we had never gone ashore to check out Winslow, the downtown area in the City of Bainbridge Island. Our yacht club had a reciprocal moorage agreement with Queen City Yacht Club. I knew this leg of my summer trip might be uncomfortable with a lot of commercial traffic and ferries that ply frequently between downtown Seattle and Bainbridge Island, as well as between Seattle and Bremerton, but I was anticipating having a good time in Winslow.

Ferry Encounter in Eagle Harbor

Ferries are big and fast; however, they have limited mobility navigating corners in confined areas. Such was the case when I approached Eagle Harbor after leaving Blake Island in August 2023. The Bainbridge to Seattle ferry is scheduled hourly, and the ferry from Seattle to Eagle Harbor in Bainbridge leaves at the same time. There was a window of opportunity of 30 minutes to navigate the long, twisting channel to reach Eagle Harbor before the ferry arrived. I began entering the harbor as the ferry left Bainbridge Island. On a previous trip to Eagle Harbor for a raft-up, I was crewing on a sailboat, and the captain took a shortcut and turned to port before we reached the turn marked with buoys. The boat ran aground on soft mud and sand. The captain tried in vain to back out using the engine. Then, he had the crew gather on one side of the boat and lean out as far as they could to lift the keel out of the mud. It worked! But the captain was embarrassed. His face was red; he had frequently lectured the crew to respect the navigation buoys. It was a good learning experience. We found out what happens if you don't follow the rules! Back on my boat, the batteries were dying, so I had to move slowly through the half mile long channel. Just as I was approaching the last turn to port and looking forward to the final dash to the marina, I heard 5 short horn blasts behind me. This is a signal used by boats hailing one another asking what the heck are you doing!? I looked around and saw the ferry from Seattle bearing down on me. So, I answered, giving the horn signal letting them know they could pass on the port side of my boat. I steered out of the channel to starboard, grimly observing the hazard buoy signifying rocks and shallow water getting closer. The ferry passed behind me, and I survived that encounter. Luckily it was daytime so the ferry could see me. I generally stay as far away from ferries as possible, but I learned a few important lessons that day. Don't let your batteries die before entering a long, tight passage and don't underestimate the speed of ferries and cargo ships.

Winslow and the City of Bainbridge Island

Winslow is the downtown area neighborhood in the heart of the City of Bainbridge Island. The city's Waterfront Park and Dock are conveniently located near stores and restaurants in Winslow. I tied up to the dock and walked up to the pay station.

Although the fees were reasonable, there was no free temporary docking. The 3-hour fee for my 30-foot boat was $3.45, and an overnight stay was $17.50 plus $5.76 for electricity. The pump out station is on the west end of the dock marked with yellow paint. The dock allows boats up to 70' depending on availability. I decided to spend 2 days there, to stock up on groceries, charge the batteries and pump out the holding tank. There was a grocery store just up the hill. It was good to walk and stretch after injuring my leg in Port Orchard. I always carry my reusable shopping bags when going shopping, and today was no exception. The market had a good selection of vegetables, so I bought a steak for the grill, potatoes, and salad makings. On the gangway back to my boat, I met a skipper who also lived aboard his boat. It was a beautiful, well maintained 38-foot wooden sloop. Back on my boat, it was good to relax and watch the sunset after a stressful day on the water. I'm amazed at the camaraderie that exists between sailors; there are no strangers around the dock! The next day I called Harbour Marina. The Bainbridge Island Yacht Club had a reciprocal agreement with my club, so I reserved a night. I still can't get over how courteous and professional all the harbormasters I've met have been, even with their responsibility for many boats and their marina infrastructure. After I moved my boat to the guest dock at Harbour marina, I took one last walk through Winslow on this warm summer evening. There were some restaurants with outside dining areas overlooking the marina. Amidst the delicious smells coming from the food, and the soft light from the restaurants, I overheard snippets of relaxed conversations from the contented diners. I would keep Winslow in mind for a future visit.

Port Madison

Leaving Eagle Harbor, I had a favorable light wind that took me all the way to Port Madison. On the approach to the channel, I noticed several boats with dive flags flying. One of the boats approached me, and the skipper advised me there was a swimmer in the water. I read a poster in Bainbridge Island earlier about the relay swimming race around Bainbridge Island, but I had no idea that I would get to see the participants. As I carefully made my way into the channel, the swimmer passed behind me. He looked tired but determined. I can only imagine how tough you had to be to swim long distances in the ocean like that! I arrived in Port Madison at the beginning of flood tide. The guide read of narrow channels and shifting mud, so I was apprehensive and kept a careful eye on my depth finder on the way in. The harbor was small and narrow, even for my boat; I thought calling it a "port" was a stretch. My destination was the Port Madison Yacht Club where my club had reciprocal mooring privileges. I had called Port Madison Yacht Club a day earlier to confirm the availability of guest moorage. As I arrived at the guest dock, I was graciously welcomed by the current commodore of the club, who told me I was welcome to use the clubhouse and grounds. The next morning, I decided to walk to the Fay Bainbridge State Park two miles away. My leg injury was feeling much better, so I enjoyed the chance to stretch my legs on the long walk with gently sloping hills. I had passed by this park from the water on my way to Port Madison. The park had a mooring ball so you could tie a boat up and take a dinghy to the beach, but I didn't see it even with binoculars as I passed by. However, I did locate the mooring ball from the beach. I made a mental note to stop there on my way to Kingston someday. The park was small, but the beach was nice with gentle waves lapping on the shore. The panoramic view of the mountains across the Sound was incredible. It wasn't like an ocean beach, but there was driftwood as far as the eye could see. As I explored, I came across a hornet's nest in a rotting piece of silvery driftwood. I gingerly stepped around it as I made my way to the south end of the park, then continued north back along the sandy beach. When I reached the north end of the park, I heard a hoarse moaning yell. I turned around and noticed a young boy screaming as he danced on the log I had recently circumvented, waving his hands violently and swatting himself. The boy had stumbled into the hornet's nest. A group of people, presumably his family, were about 50 feet from him. Several of them ran up to the child and they also started dancing around swatting themselves. I had been stung by a hornet a few weeks before and could imagine their pain and fear. I stood transfixed, watching the scene. Then, a younger individual left the main group and escorted the boy away. Then they all headed down to the water to soak the wounds from the stings. This was a reminder to me that when you are out in nature, even in a place as seemingly as innocuous as northwest Washington, you still need to be aware of your surroundings. This was the wilderness where the inhabitants would defend their home to the death.

Upon returning to the marina, I encountered another Port Madison Yacht Club member and former commodore. He was performing some plumbing maintenance on the docks, tracing a leak in the water system. I noticed there was an odor of sulfur when filling my potable water jugs the night before in the clubhouse. When I mentioned that, he educated me on the different classes of groundwater that were regulated by the state. He said if this were a class "B" water system, serving private customers, all they would have to do is aerate the water to remove the smell. "The sulfur doesn't affect the water quality", he said, "The smell comes from tiny bubbles in the water.". Because this water supply served visitors to the marina, it was classified as an "A" water system and required expensive filtering to conform to regulations. I had noticed the blackberries growing along the rural road which ran by the marina, and I commented about them. He said the Himalayan blackberries were better with a more delicate flavor, but unfortunately, the peak season for them was over. The two varieties of blackberries are easily distinguishable. Although they both have palmate leaves, the evergreen blackberry leaves are smooth, whereas the Himalayan blackberry has deeply jagged leaves. As I travel around out on my boat, I marvel at how easy it is to strike up a conversation with all the people I meet.

Port Madison to Kingston Crab Fest

I left Port Madison to arrive in Kingston in time for my yacht club's crab feed event. The Port of Kingston consists of a ferry terminal, a marina that sits behind a breakwater, and an expansive park with ramadas. There is an anchorage in the port and even a few mooring balls to the north of the ferry terminal. I tied up at an empty slip at the guest dock, then walked up to the marina office to pay the fee and get the restroom, shower, and laundry room passcodes. I took advantage of the facilities to shower and wash my clothes. While many marinas offer showers and restrooms, not all of them have laundry facilities. While I was relaxing in the park, I saw some of my fellow club members, and joined them for the crab feast. I had dropped my crab trap a few days earlier but didn't catch any keepers. None of the club members had caught any either, so we had to pitch in and buy them. They were the Dungeness variety, my favorite, although it takes a little work to break the shell to get to the succulent meat inside. I spent that night at the marina and the next day I cast off and moved to the anchorage to the south. When I asked the harbormaster about the mooring balls on the north side of the ferry terminal, he didn't recommend using them. Apparently, the severity of the ferries' wakes is so bad, they make those mooring balls unusable. I spent a couple of days anchored in the Kingston area. The first night wasn't bad, but on the second, my boat was rocked violently by the wake of one of the ferry boats. It is a beautiful spot, with good public transportation to different places on the Sound, but I will not anchor there again.

The Pirates of Poulsbo

After leaving Kingston, I decided to go to Poulsbo for Pirate Days. It is a quiet town in the northwest area of Puget Sound. Its harbor is protected on all sides from adverse weather and there is no commercial traffic. The westernmost part of the bay is shallow with a muddy bottom. Because of this and the proximity to the city marina, it is an ideal anchorage. When I arrived in Poulsbo, I rented a slip for a few nights to participate in the Pirate Days festivities. This was the first time I had visited Poulsbo. I took care of the boat's maintenance items, then went to a barbeque restaurant for supper. The next day I toured the town on foot, where I found restaurants, art galleries, real estate offices, and curio shops. I stopped for lunch at a pizzeria where they offered anchovies as a topping. I was in Heaven! On the west side of town were some houses that had been converted into museums. Poulsbo was settled by people from Scandinavia back in the day, who established logging and fishing companies. The original name submitted for the town was "Paulsbo", the name of a town in Norway, but the registrar misread it as "Poulsbo". The Marina Market, not to be confused with the Longship Marine store, is located a few short blocks just north of the city park. It has a wide selection of healthy German and Scandinavian foods. I bought some small loaves of nutritious breakfast bread, a rye bread densely packed with nuts, some crackers, canned kippered herring, and anchovies. While walking the city park paths, I found a blackberry hedge. Since it was late summer, there was an abundance of ripe berries. I picked enough to last several days. In the afternoon on this warm, perfect summer day, I heard music coming from the city park pergola. A musician had set up his electric guitar and vintage amplifier and was playing a selection of mellow old songs. He was taking requests and would sometimes change the lyrics of some of the familiar songs to reflect the locale. "Sittin' On the Dock of the Bay" was now "Liberty Bay", in that old Otis Redding song. I relaxed in the park all afternoon listening to music. Afterwards, while walking down the path to the seafood restaurant overlooking the bay, I chanced upon the commodore and friends from my yacht club. We went to supper at a nearby restaurant, and shared drinks and some great food, including steamed clams and grilled salmon. This was the 1st day of the Poulsbo Pirate Days, and it was shaping up well. The next morning, I made pancakes with blackberries and an omelet with pepper jack cheese and anchovies. For the Pirate Days festival, it was customary for attendees to don pirate gear and talk like pirates. We walked up and down the docks, visiting the parties on the boats, swilling ale and wine, and sampling hors d'oeuvres. Several skippers from SSYC were attending with their boats. Having discharged their captain duties by reaching Poulsbo safely, they were now entitled to drink as much as they could hold. One attendee fell into the water but was quickly rescued!

After the festivities, I spent a couple of lazy weeks anchored in the harbor reading novels and planning the next part of my journey. Occasionally, I would go back into town to sample restaurant food. I urge you to try the Mexican restaurant. Casa Luna is tucked into an alleyway off the main street, and the food is great! Poulsbo became one of my favorite anchorages, with its safe and secure moorage, quaint stores and good restaurants nearby. The beautiful summer days were growing shorter, and I knew I needed to sail south and find a new home for my boat for the winter. I will visit Poulsbo again next summer.

Hull Speed Observation – Poulsbo to Blake Island

Blake Island State Park had become my go-to overnight spot. It is centrally located and except for the northeast side, has mooring balls all around it. I am becoming so familiar with the island; I can find where the mooring balls are even in the middle of the night. I left Poulsbo and travelled down the channel, turning to port as I entered Rich Passage. I followed the passage until I saw Blake Island in the distance. I kept close to Manchester's shore off my starboard side. I would be out of the way there in case the Bremerton to Seattle ferry suddenly popped out from behind the bend in the channel. I saw a sailboat in the distance, probably coming from Elliot Bay across the Sound. Its sails weren't up and was under power. I assumed it would turn to its starboard and continue up Rich Passage to its destination. Although the sailboat wasn't that large, maybe a 30-

footer, its bow was high up in the air. As it drew closer, I became alarmed; the boat was not altering course or reducing speed. It was too late to evade it, but if I didn't do something soon, it would hit me. Forgetting about the 5 blasts on the signaling device that one is supposed to use to query the recipient's intention, I leaned on the horn. I had bought the horn at an auto parts store and mounted it high on the mast. It was very loud, and the other boat's skipper heard it. He poked his head above the bow of his boat with a surprised look, then quickly went back to the cockpit and spun the boat to starboard to avoid colliding with me or the shore. I believe he was lucky I was there, otherwise he would have surely grounded his boat on the rocky shore on my starboard side. Yes, I did have the right-of-way in that encounter. A vessel's "hull speed" for a displacement type hull isn't necessarily its top speed. His boat had to be doing at least 20 knots. I can only imagine what kind of motor was in that boat for it to go that fast. Who says a displacement sailboat can't plane!

Between Two Ferries

I spent the night moored at Blake Island and planned my next day's journey back to my slip at Foss Harbor Marina in Tacoma. The wind was forecast to be up to 5 knots from the north. The shortest distance to Tacoma was via Colvos Passage. I usually took this route to Blake Island because the current in the passage tended to go north, independent of the tides. There was also no commercial traffic in Colvos Passage, except for an occasional barge. But today, the wind wouldn't be strong enough to complete the passage back to Tacoma via that passage. So, I decided to go around the east side of Vashon Island. In the morning, I hoisted the sails and cast off. There is a commercial ferry from Fauntleroy to Vashon Island, then to Southworth on the mainland west of Seattle. This is a busy route with 2 ferries leaving approximately every 30 minutes from each side, crossing next to each other a few hundred yards apart to the east of Vashon Island. Before making that crossing, I studied the schedule and picked a time where I would be out of their way as I was making my way perpendicular to their path. I always give ferry boats a wide berth. They are very fast and leave a big wake that can make a sailor uncomfortable. I had left Blake Island catching an optimistic breeze that would surely take me through that area quickly. Unfortunately, the wind died as it is prone to do when you are counting on it. I turned on the motor and started cruising south as fast as practicable, needing to keep some reserve in case I needed power later. It wasn't fast enough. I wasn't worried because technically I had the right of way, and my boat was easily seen. One ferry went north of me and the other south of me by 100 yards. I knew from previous experience to meet the wakes from boats on the front or rear corners of my boat, which is what happened. But instead of both ends going up at the same time and the waves passing harmlessly underneath, my boat ended up rocking violently from side to side and fore to aft. Fortunately, the boat didn't ship any water over the sides of the hull. It was experiences like this that made me trust my tough little boat.

Des Moines Yacht Club Potluck and Pyrotechnics Display

On my way back from the north Puget Sound to my home marina in Tacoma, I had been bucking a southerly wind and had to use my electric motor to make any headway. I looked at the map and saw that the Des Moines marina and the Saltwater State Park were on the way. I needed electric power but didn't want to pay the entire fee for guest moorage at the marina. I looked at my list of marinas and saw that the Des Moines Yacht Club had their own dock at that marina. I called, and the phone was answered by the Commodore of the yacht club. She welcomed me to their dock, which was the southernmost one at the marina. When she met me at the dock to give me the keys to the gate and collect the electricity fee for the night, she invited me up for a potluck dinner. When I said I didn't have anything to bring, she said to come up anyway, "There's plenty of food". Back at the boat I found a can of gourmet baked beans and heated them up. It was a good contribution as there weren't any other baked beans at the barbeque. I joined the folks in line, who wondered who I was, so I introduced myself and told them which yacht club I represented. After dressing a hamburger and scooping some potato salad and beans, I joined the festivities. As twilight arrived, the commodore announced a demonstration of pyrotechnic devices. We gathered around the speaker, a Coast Guard retiree. He discussed the different types of visual emergency signals, including flare guns, handheld flares, and electronic beacons. He exhibited a handheld smoke flare, useful for daytime signaling, and educated us on which circumstances and conditions to use the various flares. He also illustrated the difference between devices used on commercial craft versus small pleasure boats. Flares on commercial boats are much larger and last for a longer time. The Coast Guard requires that the flares on a boat must not have passed their expiration date, and he wrapped up the demonstration by passing out flare guns and expired flares to shoot up into the air. "I got permission from the Coast Guard", he said, "It's illegal to shoot these off unless you have an actual emergency". The demonstration was effective. Flares aren't very noticeable during daytime hours. I didn't have any of the orange smoke flares on board, so I picked some up the next time I was at a marine supply store. You can't be too safe.

CHAPTER 19: FINDING A NEW MARINA

My plan, after relinquishing my mooring slip at Foss Harbor Marina and spending the summer sailing and exploring, was to find a spot to moor my boat for the winter and get a small storage unit in the South Sound area. Although everything I owned would now either fit into my boat or in my panel van, I needed a storage unit to keep my off-season clothes in. During my online research, I found some marinas on Budd Bay in the Olympia area, Boston Harbor Marina, Percival Landing, Swantown Marina, and West Bay Marina.

Leaving Des Moines, I landed at the Foss Waterway Seaport Museum public dock. It was close to Foss Harbor Marina and my current storage garage. I have been to the museum several times to read about Foss Harbor's history and look at the wooden boats. The large warehouse was available for weddings, receptions, and small concerts. Sometimes I would listen to the concerts while on my way to the "Rock the Dock" bar and restaurant just on the other side of the museum. My favorite meal at Rock the Dock was their black and blue bacon cheeseburger. I loaded the rest of my tools, parts, and belongings into the van, and went to the marina office to turn in my keys for the deposit. They allowed me to park my van in one of the temporary parking spots to make it a less likely target for theft. I would be back in a few days to fetch the van and say goodbye. The next day, as I was preparing to cast off from the museum dock, a family with several children came down the gangway armed with fishing poles. The Coho salmon enter

Puget Sound every other year to find their spawning grounds. There are millions of fish, and they are all hungry. I spoke to the family, and they told me they were from the Ukraine. The father caught a salmon right away. I'm sure they were happy to be in Washington instead of in the war.

I called Boston Harbor first. Unfortunately, they didn't have any permanent moorage available for large boats. They did, however, have an open space to moor on their guest dock. So, I cast off from the public dock and left Foss Harbor for Olympia. I stopped by at the Narrows Marina the first night. It's on the east side as you pass under the bridge going south. The current is strong there, so be careful when navigating to an available slip. The guest slips all have a "Reserved" sign. They are for any guest who pays for their moorage. There is another temporary parking dock for guests at one of the two restaurants at the marina. As you walk down the dock to the pay station, you will encounter a bait fish farm covered by a nylon net. The net is there to keep the seagulls and herons from stealing the fish. There is a good restaurant, as well as a brewery and dance hall at this marina. I treated myself to a nice supper and spent some time relaxing in the pleasant surroundings. I didn't know of this marina during my first trip under the Narrows Bridge, otherwise I could have stayed there instead of motoring around Fox Island all night. I should have researched my first trip better. But then I would have missed out on a beautiful moonlight sail and making friends with a sea lion.

The next stop would be the mooring balls at Tolmie State Park. To get there, I would have to transit north above the Nisqually Reach. This was a large area of mud flats and an aquatic reserve managed by the Department of Natural Resources. Although I had driven by Nisqually Flats a hundred times on I-5 while going to visit family members who lived in Oregon, this was the first time I had sailed by it from the other side. I had never stopped to see the reserve, it looked interesting. There was a raised platform where you could view the wildlife and it was popular with migrating birds. I vowed to stop at the reserve in the future. Although there was a good steady wind from the northeast on the way to Tolmie State Park, it was dark when I arrived. I spent a few minutes with my spotlight to find one of the five mooring balls. They were right where I expected them to be according to the marine travel guide. I only stayed the evening there, but the amenities of the park included a saltwater diving spot. I would have to return one day with friends and explore this park further. This was the furthest south I have travelled on Puget Sound, so everything around here was new to me. I liked the fact there was very little commercial traffic. I saw a small barge once in the distance, and only a few other boats like mine. The next day I would wait for the tide to help push my boat through Henderson Inlet, then turn to port and go through Dana Passage to reach Boston Harbor.

Boston Harbor Marina is nestled in a small cove on a point on the northeast side of the entrance to Budd Bay. As I walked along the dock to the office to pay for the night, there was the smell of fried fish coming from their snack bar. I rarely eat fried food, and never while on the water. It would be bad to have boiling oil sloshing around on a propane burner. It smelled so good; I read their snack bar menu and treated myself to the fried cod and sweet potato fries. The codfish was golden crunchy perfection and the sweet potato fries were exemplary, crisp on the outside and creamy on the inside. Sometimes on my trips I would come across neighborhood free lending libraries. They were usually a box mounted on a short post like a mailbox, with a glass door and a birdhouse roof to keep the books from getting wet. Sometimes I would find them at intersections on the rural roads near a bus stop, and almost always at marinas. Most of the books were fluff fiction novels, but sometimes I would find a useful non-fiction book. I would take the book back to my boat and replace it with another from my shelf. I am really loving this retirement lifestyle, taking each day, and savoring it, and in no hurry to be somewhere at a certain time! After reading a few pages, I fell asleep. The next day would be a quick day of sailing, then I could start exploring the marinas in the Olympia area.

I read about Swantown Marina in my travel guide and checked it out online. It's a large, modern marina, a little more expensive, but with the benefit of having a haul out service nearby. I would need to take my boat out of the water before next season to put a new coat of antifouling marine paint on and check out the propeller shaft play. Unfortunately, because I had so many problems with theft and vandalism with my car while at Foss Harbor Marine in downtown Tacoma, I was leery of parking my car in an area with easy access or near high crime areas.

As I sailed towards Olympia, I called the closest marina, which was West Bay Marina. When researching marinas in Olympia, I was intrigued by a quote on the marina's web site," Sailboats attract the loons and geniuses among us, the romantics whose boats represent some outlaw image of themselves. We fall for these things, but what we're slow to grasp is that it's not the boats but rather those inexplicable moments on the water where time slows. The entire industry is built on a feeling, an emotion." — Before the Wind by Olympia's own Jim Lynch.

After getting my dock slip assignment, I pulled into the marina and moored at the guest dock. I noticed a large, two-story building on the shore. The upper floor was a restaurant called Annie's. It is an older marina, somewhat run down, but relatively cheap compared to modern, updated marinas. Newer marinas have composite wood/plastic decking on the floating docks and solid aluminum corrugated mesh on ramps. The floating docks at Westbay Marina look to be covered in plywood siding. Gingerly picking my way to the office to pay for the night, I had to be careful of where I stepped. There was some rotting wood, soft spots, and slime. This dock was mostly sheltered with a corrugated metal roof, and housed motorboats, as well as a bait fish farm. There was a slight but pervasive odor of decomposing clams and sea otter excrement at low tide. I saw a few derelict boats on the way; someone's dream once, but abandoned now, and quietly deteriorating. At the office I inquired about permanent moorage. The dockmaster on duty said there was. I decided then to take the moorage. It would save me hundreds of dollars over the winter, and I reasoned that I could easily find other moorage after next summer's sailing season. As I was leaving, after paying for the first and last month's moorage, the harbormaster said "Oh, yeah, no liveaboards". In Washington State, you are not considered a liveaboard unless you spend 15 or more days per month at a marina. As I intended to spend as much time on the water as possible, and stay with my family during the winter, I could abide by this. As a bonus, after I changed my residential address for my auto insurance, it went down $10 per month! The marina had a pump out, restrooms, a laundry area, and shower facilities located under the restaurant. The two showers in the men's room were out of order. It appeared they were in the process of being remodeled and had been for months. There was another shower between the restrooms. I looked in and noticed mud and water on the tile floor. I made a note to get rubber shoes or flip-flops for the shower. I've been fortunate to never have had athlete's foot fungus and didn't want to get it now. The marina was at the end of a road and shared its parking lot with the restaurant. Nobody would drive or walk down that road unless they had business there. I felt that my van would be much safer there than at Foss Harbor. Indeed, after several months, my van hasn't been vandalized. My new marina, at $1.00 per foot plus a flat fee for electricity, was a bargain.

CHAPTER 20: GOODBYE, FOSS HARBOR

I needed to fetch my van that I had left at Foss Harbor Marina and bring it to my new marina. I walked about a mile into downtown Olympia to catch the intercity bus to Tacoma. To my surprise, I found that Olympia's busses were free of charge. After the ride to Tacoma's south side park and ride, I transferred to a local bus and used my Orca card to complete the trip to downtown Tacoma. Downtown Tacoma is built up on a hill, probably 100 feet above sea level. Fortunately, you can walk down 11th street to the east, towards the bridge, and find an elevator that will save you many steps to reach the waterfront. From the elevator, I walked to Foss Harbor to pick up my van. I said my goodbyes to the office staff and a few of my neighbors, then drove my van to its new home in Olympia.

Meeting the New Neighbors

Now that I had secured a mooring spot for the winter, I relaxed for a few days and met my new neighbors. My next-door neighbor worked in the Army. His job was in logistics. That was a coincidence, as I spent some of my career doing much the same with supply chain automation. I spoke to my other neighbors down the pier. They had a young chocolate Labrador dog. It wasn't a puppy by any means, but he was still adjusting to his gangly adolescence. One day, I saw a new boat dock in an empty slip a few boats away. It was a smaller 27-foot boat and the boat's name was "Mr Blue Sky". Who doesn't love that Electric Light Orchestra song? I always smile whenever I see that boat pull in. I met the family who owned it. They were new to sailing and spent hours honing their skills and enjoying their new boat! While walking around the docks one day, I saw another boat that looked like my Rawson. The neighbor was at home, so I asked her about the boat. It was indeed a Rawson 30 but was built in 1980. I could see several changes made to the design over the years from my 1960 boat. The improvements included a bowsprit that moved the jib halyard forward to improve handling, and a built-in windlass to pull the anchor up.

Percival Landing

I wanted to explore Olympia's downtown area. I could dock at Percival Landing, Olympia's city dock and walk from there. One day I made the trip to Percival Landing and tied up to the city dock. Temporary mooring was free for up to 4 hours on dock "E", and there is metered parking available nearby. A pump out station is conveniently located to the port side as you enter the landing. The maximum stay is 7 days in a 30-day period. You can check the Percival Landing website for updated information. As I toured the cute, vibrant downtown area, I noticed my bank had a branch here. I stopped at a bar to have a burger. Then I checked out the used book and video stores to get some reading and viewing material for those relaxing hours on the hook. I enjoyed the Olympia area, with its many amenities within walking distance. Some of the shops had awnings to keep the rain or sun off pedestrians, and many of the roads had bike routes marked. There was a large park bordering the lake near the state capitol building that also had bike routes. Yes, I think I will like it here, and so will my bicycle.

CHAPTER 21:
HALLOWEEN 2023

Halloween was approaching rapidly, and I had been invited to a friend's annual party. It was an hour-long trip from Olympia to Kent, Washington, where the party was held. Even though that was a long way to drive, I hadn't seen my friends and fellow yacht club members for a while. I wondered what I would do for my costume for this year. I thought about the experiences I had during this summer of sailing, and an idea popped into my head. While sailing one day in Case Inet, I saw the bloated carcass of something in the water. As I got nearer, I could tell that it was a sea lion. It had old white propeller scars on its back. They had healed long before whatever had killed it recently. That sight really spoke to me. I had a wetsuit with dark brown, black, and dull green mottled colors that kind of looked like sea lion skin. I also had two sets of flippers. They were black and blue, so I covered the blue with a black permanent marker. I donned the wet suit and duct taped the flippers on my arms and legs. I added some strips of white tape to the back of the wet suit to emulate the propeller scars. I wore a black balaclava on my head to complete the look, and for good measure, I wrapped a fish net around me like a shawl. The costume would be perfect! I felt bad about the many marine mammals killed by being hit by propellers or trapped in fishing nets, and I take every opportunity I can to raise awareness of their plight and to promote the environment. It was easy to dance in the costume, and it was a hit. I tied for first place in the men's costume category, and I even voted for the other guy!

CHAPTER 22:
ONE MORE TRIP
BEFORE WINTER

After spending a week at the dock in my new marina in Olympia waiting out some damp weather, I got bored. The weather was mild, and I had time for another 2-week sailing trip before heading down to Oregon to join my family for Thanksgiving. I had read about Jarrell Cove State Park and drove around Harstine Island once to visit it. Harstine Island has a lot of cool places, including tidal pools, to explore. So, I provisioned up and set out. I stopped at Boston Harbor the first night and waited for favorable tides the next day that would slingshot me through Dana Passage, to the south of Harstine Island. I would take the passage to Case Inlet on the east side, then I would sail up and around to the west to reach Jarrell Cove. There is a shorter route on the west side, near Squaxin Island, but there is a bridge that joins Harstine Island with the mainland. Although I drove over the bridge many years ago, I couldn't remember how high it was. I figured I could check out the bridge from the north from Jarrell Cove.

The next day, I made my way to Joemma State Park and tied up to one of their mooring balls. Another goal while making my way to Olympia was to check out all the state park mooring spots in the South Puget Sound. This was mainly a cursory inspection; I didn't have a lot of time to spend at each one, but I would reference each moorage for further exploration or as a place to stay while sailing to other destinations. While there was an abundance of mooring balls here at Joemma State Park, they were only sheltered from wind and waves from the north and east sides. Staying there would not be comfortable with high winds from the south. However, it looked like there were some interesting features on land, including a bridge, and would be worth a kayak trip to explore. That evening, I noticed something I hadn't seen for a while. With all the bright lights of the Seattle metropolitan area, I rarely saw stars in the sky, but tonight they were dazzling in the clear, dry air.

In the morning, I navigated across Case Inlet to McMicken Island. I had read about this island, which was just off the east side of Harstine Island, about halfway up. It would be another good place to spend the night. The tiny island looked so beautiful, I took my kayak to the shore and explored it. The travel guide said the shallow strait between the islands was a good place to harvest oysters and clams. Because I was in a hurry to reach Jarrell Cove, I left the oysters unmolested.

Jarrell Cove State Park

Jarrell Cove State Park is located just west of the northern tip of Harstine Island in Puget Sound, Washington. It offers a 60' dock for pumping out your boat or unloading passengers, 14 mooring balls, and a separate dock with electricity on the south end of the cove. I have heard that this park is crowded during the summer, but here in November, there was only one other boat tied up to a mooring ball. I used the pump out and walked up the hill to register for a mooring ball. If you pay cash, or have the annual mooring permit, you can just fill out the envelope and slip it into the box. Otherwise, you need to see the park campground host to use a credit card. I saw a couple of employees working in the park, and met Jim, the campground host. We chatted for a while. He told me stories of his hosting experience, most recently at the North Cascades State Park. He had been driving his new trailer around and camped in the

North Cascades State Park, where he was offered an unexpected campground host opportunity. I had recently read about a new gold discovery near the town of Republic, Washington, which was in that area. I carry a gold pan and a collapsible shovel around in my van and try my luck whenever travelling and camping in gold country. I recently found out that my brother-in-law was a gold hound, too, so we made plans to try our luck and find some gold while camping in various areas next summer. The campground host had indeed heard about the discovery in the North Cascades and gave me some tips on where to look for gold! We discussed moorage, and he recommended that I tie up at the south dock that had electricity hookups. Since I had the mooring permit, he would only charge me the $6 fee for electricity. I would use this opportunity to top off my batteries, especially since the forecast called for cloudy and rainy weather. The restrooms at this campground were very clean, heated, and I took advantage of the free shower. On the way back to the boat, I noticed some huckleberry bushes loaded with fruit, so I picked some for my pancakes. The maximum stay is 3 days in a row, so I cocooned and read while waiting out some rainy weather. I could spend the rest of my life like this!

The Port of Allyn, WA

After a couple of weeks on the water, I decided one day to do my laundry. The closest town was Allyn, Washington. I didn't see any laundromats in Allyn on Google Maps, but I hoped there would be one near the town. I was also running out of eggs and creamer for my coffee. For some reason, I was also craving a soda. I checked the weather forecast as I left Jarrell Cove for Allyn. The wind would be steady from the south at 10 mph. I left Jarrell Cove, hoisted the sails, and landed at Allyn's city park dock. After securing the boat, I went up the hill to the pay station. The sign said that mooring was free from 7AM to 7PM. Overnight moorage was $1.50 per foot per night between June 1 and September 30 and $10 for electricity, or $9.50 per foot per month from October 1 to April 30. Electricity was an additional $50 per month. It didn't list overnight fees for the remainder of the year between October 1st and May 31st. This was confusing. I didn't know if there was a charge for overnight mooring in the off season. I went up to the office. Only one person was working, and she didn't know either. She picked up the phone and called the office manager. Evidently, they never receive visitors in the off-season. The electricity was also off. It had been turned off after some sea otters vandalized the power lines to the dock months earlier but hadn't been repaired yet. I left the office with instructions to use the pay station and pay the summer rate. I noticed a gas station and a burger joint across the street from the park. The lady in the office raved about the hamburger joint, so I had one. I don't get hamburger very often while living on my boat, but there was nothing special about this one. I satisfied my soda craving there and went next door to the gas station convenience store for half and half for my coffee. The prices were very high. Beverages were $2.86 for a 16oz bottle, and they didn't have any half and half. After looking up and down the street, I didn't see a laundromat. So, I checked the bus schedule to Belfair, which was the nearest town. The fare was free, but I didn't feel right about taking my dirty laundry on the bus. Some cities were beginning to regulate what you can bring on a bus. Like shopping carts and garbage bags. I had hoped to see the Hood Canal side of Puget Sound while I was in Belfair but felt that the laundry would have been an impediment. After I bought my supplies, it was starting to drizzle, so I hopped on the bus going back to Allyn. A block later, the bus stopped for a homeless dude. As he dragged his sleeping bag up the stairs with one hand while holding a tall cup of Starbucks coffee in the other, the bus driver asked him if he needed help boarding. She even offered to hold his coffee! Now, I think it would be OK to take my laundry around on public transportation. Oh, and I got to see Hood Canal from the bus!

The Storm in Allyn

The wind was growing steadily from the south, and it started to rain while I ran my errands in Belfair. A storm was brewing. By the time I got back to my boat at the city dock in Allyn, I had to decide whether to stay at the dock for the night or take off and anchor nearby to ride the storm out. The charts and travel guide I used for the trip showed that the bay to the north outside Allyn was a large shallow mud flat at low tide. Since the wind was coming from the south, I felt there was a risk the high wind and waves could pull the anchor up, stranding me on the mud flat.

I decided to spend the night tied up to the dock. I double checked the mooring lines as the rain grew heavier, then went inside the cabin. I hoped the wind would die down, as it often does in the evenings on Puget Sound. Evening came and the wind, instead of abating, kept getting stronger. I had eaten the hamburger earlier, so I didn't have to prepare food on the boat. The waves started to grow higher, and the boat started heaving. I took a meclizine tablet for seasickness and put my foul weather gear on. Sailors call them "foulies". They are very good to have when sailing in wet, windy weather. I made sure that my backpack was ready to go, and a life jacket was handy, in case the boat started to founder and sink. The rocking of the boat was making me increasingly uncomfortable, and I needed to get some sleep. At around 11:00 PM, I jumped from the boat to the dock, then walked up to the park to find a place to sleep. I came to a large, covered ramada with picnic tables. It offered shelter from the rain, but not from the chilly wind, and I couldn't see the boat from the ramada. It was dark when I went back towards the dock and found a bench with a canopy and trellis that kept most of the rain and wind off. I laid down to get some rest as the storm continued. After what seemed like hours, but was more likely a few minutes, I went back down the dock to check on the boat. It was bucking and heaving like a wild horse at the end of a tether! I was afraid it would smash itself to pieces on the dock, so I crawled to the other side of the boat, retrieved an unused fender, and placed it between the boat and dock. I had to time the operation just right so I wouldn't get my hand or arm crushed. Then I went forward and took the mooring line I used when tying up to a ball and draped it over the bow pulpit rail so I could reach it from the dock. I exited the boat by throwing myself on the dock, then picked up the mooring line and secured it to a cleat on the dock in front of the boat. "There", I said to myself as the boat's violent motion eased up. I was exhausted by then, but warm and dry in my foul weather gear. I went back up to the park bench and drifted off to sleep.

By morning, the storm had passed, and the sun was rising in the partly cloudy sky. I went down to the dock to examine my boat for damage. The hull appeared intact, although the rub rail was broken and missing in places. Some of the paint on the side of the hull under the fenders had rubbed off. Two of the three mooring lines were hanging on by threads. Even though I had wrapped reinforcing cloth around the lines where they met the rub rail, the continual abrasion and stress had nearly worn them through. I followed the rigging up with my eyes and saw that the windvane was missing from the top of the mast. When I came aboard, I found the windvane lying in the bottom of the cockpit. The wind and waves had been so strong and violent, they had broken the sturdy fiberglass windvane mount. I was fortunate that the windvane fell in the boat. By all rights, it should have blown into the water. I figured I could save some money and repair and reinforce the mount with epoxy glue and a layer or two of fiberglass. I needed to haul the boat out to dry dock in the springtime and refresh the antifouling paint; I could touch up the damaged paint on the side where the fenders had damaged it. After this experience, I concluded I might have been better off anchoring out on the mud flats, rather than tying the boat to the dock. I will try that the next time.

CHAPTER 23:
POTABLE WATER

From Allyn, I sailed back to Jarrell Cove State Park for a well-deserved rest and a shower. I tied up at the dock and charged up my drive and house batteries. The days were getting shorter and cloudier, and it was time to go to my home marina for the winter. The next morning, I stopped at the fuel station at Jarrell's Cove Marina across the channel to fill the water tank. As I glided up to the dock, a man with a giant mustache ran down the pier to assist with mooring. "It's electric drive", I said, as I fine-tuned the approach. "I noticed that", he smiled, "There are a couple of them in this marina.". I asked if there was water on the dock. "Yes, it's potable water", he smiled, twirling his mustache. I filled the water tank as he went back inside to warm up. The return trip to Boston Harbor was quick and uneventful, and I docked for the night. Later that evening after supper, I turned on the water to do my dishes. An evil, sulfurous odor emanated from the faucet. I can only imagine that the well was so deep, it tapped into one of the layers of hell. "Potable" is evidently not the same as "drinkable"! The next day, I had good wind and tides to take me back to my new home at West Bay Marina. From there I would drive to visit my family over the winter holidays. I was done with sailing for the year.

CHAPTER 24: GETTING AROUND THE SOUND ON LAND

I find it necessary to go ashore once every week or two for supplies, do my laundry, and run errands. I discovered this is possible and economical by taking advantage of public transit. While docking at various harbors in Puget Sound, I found public transportation options everywhere. In Kingston, for example, a bus will take you from the ferry terminal to a shopping center a few miles away. In Poulsbo, a bus will take you from the tourist area downtown to the grocery stores and mini malls a mile away. There are interconnections between the busses from each town, making it possible to go anywhere around the Sound very inexpensively. Some of the busses are free, and the remainder of public transportation options in the Puget Sound region, including ferries, can be paid for by using the reloadable ORCA card. ORCA stands for "One Regional Card for All". It was introduced in 2009 to allow seamless travel across different transit systems in the area, including buses, ferries, and light rail. I bought an ORCA transit card many years ago for commuting to work from the ORCA website. You can also purchase them from local transportation offices.

CHAPTER 25: SAFETY, LAWS, AND RULES

Boats can be dangerous. Water can be dangerous. Accumulated mistakes can be deadly. Humans aren't designed to live in an aquatic environment. Although humans have huge brains, they are weak, and can be damaged or drowned easily. Read and gain as much information as you can on keeping safe while boating. The state of Washington, for instance, requires recreational boaters to complete an online boating course and carry a Washington State Boater Education Card. More information on this can be found on the parks.wa.gov website. Other Washington State Vessel Laws can be found at https://app.leg.wa.gov/rcw/default.aspx?cite=79A.60. I recommend getting "A Boaters Guide to the Federal Requirements for Recreational Boats". You can download a PDF copy at https://uscgboating.org/assets/1/AssetManager/Boaters-Guide-to-Federal-Requirements-for-Receational-Boats-20231108.pdf. Other readily available books detail navigation rules, emergency signaling and what kind of flares and communications devices are required. There is a handbook called "COLREGS". It contains the international rules of the road to avoid boat collisions while navigating at sea. These rules were adopted by the United States Coast Guard, and you can either buy a hard copy or download the free PDF from the internet. It can be found at https://www.navcen.uscg.gov/sites/default/files/pdf/navRules/Nav Rules Handbook_27OCT2022_85 FR 58268.pdf. This booklet is required to be on boats over a certain length. The person who does your annual Coast Guard safety inspection will be thrilled that you have a copy of COLREGS on board. There is another link for navigation rules between sailboats: https://wow.uscgaux.info/Uploads_wowII/095-45-01/Rules_of_the_Road_for_Sailboats.pdf.

Learn how to use your VHF radio and what to communicate to the Coast Guard during emergencies. Newer marine radios have a feature called the Maritime Mobile Service Identity (MMSI) number. It is a unique 9-digit number that is assigned to a (Digital Selective Calling) DSC VHF radio. You can get this number from Boat US or other providers and program it into your radio. When you sign up for the MMSI number, you provide your boat's size, type, color, your name, address, contact information, and emergency contact information. The information provided is transferred into the U.S. Coast Guard's national distress database. On my radio, there is a "distress" button you can press in emergencies, and it will give the Coast Guard information that can help identify and locate your boat. Some VHF radios can broadcast AIS. AIS means "Automatic Identification System" and can display your boat's position to other boats with equipment to receive AIS signals. AIS is optional for most recreational boats but required for commercial ships. AIS displays will give your boat's position, speed, and direction. You can buy AIS software or hardware if you want to see locations and speeds of commercial traffic or other AIS compliant boats. You can get more information on MMSI and AIS at https://navcen.uscg.gov/ or Wikipedia. VHF radio Channel 16 is used for emergency communications with the Coast Guard and other vessels. The Coast Guard also uses this channel to announce navigation restrictions, like when the Navy is testing torpedoes, target practicing, or if submarines will be in the area. While it's permissible to use Channel 16 for a "radio check" it is preferrable to use Channel 9. You may use Channel 16 to hail another boat and let them know which channel to switch for your conversation, to keep this channel clear for emergencies. I recommend keeping a cheat sheet attached to your radio listing what information the Coast Guard will need, and letting your crew know it's there in case you are incapacitated, so they can make the call. Some of the things the Coast Guard may need are description and name of your boat, your location including the latitude and longitude, and how many persons are aboard. If you see or hear of a boat in distress in your area, you should help them if doing so will not endanger you or your crew. Depending on your location, this is the law, and in others, it is an unwritten rule. Check the rules and regulations for your area. As a captain, you are responsible for keeping yourself and your crew safe.

Ensure that your boat has appropriate signaling devices and learn when and how to use them. Freon horns are cheap and very loud. When using them, hold them far enough away from your (and other's) ears to avoid hearing loss. Alert your crew you're going to use it, so it won't startle them. Keep enough fire extinguishers onboard for the size of your boat. Put reminders on your calendar when to replace your flares and fire extinguishers when they reach their expiration date. Take time to practice emergency drills like man overboard (MOB) scenarios with your crew. These exercises can be fun, and a good team building exercise, and can save lives. Before leaving the dock, assign duties to your crew and don't yell at them. If your boat is too big for your crew to hear your outside voice, consider using portable radios. I have heard of some couples breaking up after boating trips because they think their partner is yelling at them. Don't pilot a boat under the influence of alcohol or drugs. It's OK to return to port if you experience adverse weather conditions. Teach your crew a few of the most practical knots, how to handle lines safely, what the different buoys mean, and how to pilot the boat in case you are incapacitated. If you are new to sailing, please take advantage of free or low-cost lessons offered by sailing or outdoor clubs. My yacht club, Seattle Singles Yacht Club (https://www.seattlesinglesyc.com/), often works with the Seattle branch of The Mountaineers organization to provide sailing lessons and opportunities. You can find more information at https://www.mountaineers.org/locations-lodges/seattle-branch.

When leaving on a trip, file a float plan with responsible friends, so they will know what to do and what general location you're in if you are overdue to return. Use common sense and don't leave the shore if you aren't feeling well or if your boat isn't up for the trip or weather conditions. Boat insurance usually provides for towboat services. Some insurance providers even have a cell phone app you can use to request a towboat. Keep this towboat service number handy near your marine radio.

Be aware of the weather forecast and listen to the NOAA (National Oceanic and Atmospheric Administration) station on your VHF radio. Keep in mind that weather forecasts can be wrong. Conditions on the water can be quite different than on land. Be prepared and have appropriate clothing for a range of weather conditions. Dress in layers. It's usually colder on the water, and wind speeds can be twice as strong as on land. There aren't any trees there to slow the wind down. Higher wind can bring higher waves, especially when the wind is blowing against tidal currents. Even if you sail often, refresh your memory from time to time. Your crew will respect you and admire you for explaining things in a cogent manner. Don't forget to apply sunscreen, and wear hats and long sleeves to avoid sunburn. Wear good quality sunglasses. They not only make you look cool but can also prevent cataracts. Most of the time on the water, you won't have any problems. But when you do, that's not the time to pick up a book. Sailing can be risky, but if you take precautions and know the rules, you will enjoy your time on the water even more. You earned it!

CHAPTER 26: NAVIGATION TIPS – WEATHER AND TIDES

When travelling on the sea, sailors are subject to the whimsey of the wind and weather. Tides, however, being controlled by the moon and sun, are very predictable. So much so, in fact, there are books that publish the tide tables a year in advance. The times of high and low tides change somewhat depending on how far they are from the ocean and the topography of the land under the water. I buy the tide forecast book every year. Printed on water resistant pages, I keep the book in the cockpit as I travel. It's a lot better to spread this book out on the deck than to expose your cell phone or laptop to the elements. However, I do keep my cell phone in a waterproof bag close to me in a jacket pocket. Google maps doesn't tell you much about the water you're in, however, I use it from time to time to locate landmarks. When navigating I always take advantage of the tides. They can add several knots to your speed when going with it. If the wind is good and steady, it can overcome travelling against the tide, but if it is poor or variable, I count on the tides and motor to get me to my destination. I always plan for different scenarios to have alternate, safe places to moor at the end of the day. My sailing club often hosts events at different destinations on Puget Sound. I will attend them if I'm reasonably close, but I might start a day or 2 early to make sure I get there on time. I am always happy if my trip coincides with my yacht club activities!

Bad Trips - Danger and Experience

Sailing during the summer in the warm, typically dry Pacific Northwest, while exploring the endless islands, bays, and parks, is blissful. Any wind you have during the day can die in the afternoon or evening and leave you sitting in the middle of a bay. This is the time to break out the picnic and relax on the water, although you should keep a lookout for other boat traffic. However, the weather can suddenly change. I always check the weather app on my cellphone and listen to the NOAA weather forecast on my marine VHF radio before setting off on my boat. However, the forecast is just a gaze into a crystal ball. I have had more than one experience with the wind at twice the forecasted speed. The wind blows faster on water than on land; there are no trees to slow it down. On land, the difference between 10 mph and 30 mph, while noticeable, is not life threatening. However, on the water, this can be the difference between a brisk sail and all you can handle! The NOAA weather forecasted wind speed is measured in "knots". A knot is a unit of measure used by sailors and is 1.15 times a mile. So, not a huge difference to begin with, but more significant at higher speeds. The force of the wind on your sails quadruples as the wind speed doubles. Sailing is very pleasant and comfortable with winds of 5 to 10 knots. Between 10 and 15 knots it can get challenging. When it hits 25 knots or more, and the wind is blowing the sea into a frenzy with high waves and whitecaps, it can be terrifying. Especially when sailing single-handedly. I experienced my first windstorm while sailing north from Blake Island to Shilshole Marina, just to the northwest of Seattle. Once docked at Shilshole, I planned to walk a couple of blocks to the Elks Club, where I would attend an event with my sailing club. When I cast off, a 5-knot wind was coming from the west, which I expected from the marine radio forecast. The wind started building steadily for the next 30 minutes, increasing to 10 knots, and changed direction. It was now coming from the north. Realizing that it would take all day to reach Shilshole Marina, I decided to turn south and take the wind back to my home port in Tacoma. I had both the jib and the mainsail up and anticipated a quick trip south. But the wind steadily increased to 20 knots with gusts to 35 knots. The seas were growing to 4 feet, and whitecaps were appearing on the crest of the waves. Looking around, I saw a motorboat being towed. On the VHF marine radio, I heard of other boats in trouble. Then I saw another boat, a sailboat this time, being towed. I thought briefly about calling a towboat for myself. But that would be considered a rescue operation and would have incurred a higher rate by the towing company. Although I was a little nervous, everything was under control, and I was holding my own in the southbound commercial shipping lane. Being in the shipping lane, I looked behind me frequently as cargo ships are very fast and can sneak up on you. I didn't want to be in their way, obviously. Then I spied a tugboat in the distance pushing a barge and slowly gaining on me. I sailed on, hoping to make it around the southeast corner of Maury Island, where the lee side of the island would give me some protection from the wind. The minutes dragged on. As the barge came nearer, I realized I wasn't going to make it in time. I pulled into a cove, Tramp Harbor, and waited for the tug to go by. I was sheltered from the wind here in this small area, and I had a few moments to catch my breath. In retrospect, I should have stayed there and waited for the wind to relent. But I wanted to get home. The barge passed by, and I loosened the mainsail sheet to ease my way back into the wind. As I pulled back out into the maelstrom, my mainsail violently swung to the starboard side, and the car that held the boom in place tore off the traveler slide. I hadn't loosened the mainsail enough. At the same time, the jib got tangled up in the shrouds. The wind must have been at 30 knots now. I managed to get the mainsail back under control and slid the car back onto the traveler. But now that the mainsail was back in service, I couldn't let go of the tiller to reach the jib sail and untangle it. Nor could I reach the VHF radio or my cell phone which were inside the boat. I had a portable VHF radio transmitter but had forgotten to take it out of the oven and put it in the cockpit. I kept sensitive electronics in the oven which would act as a Faraday cage, keeping the electronics safe in case of lightning or an EMP bomb. The only thing I could do was to manage the tiller and mainsail and wait for the wind to die down. I had my life jacket on, thankfully, but I was getting stressed out by the storm. I began thinking about the next steps if I lost control of my boat. I even thought about jumping overboard and swimming to shore, but remembered reading somewhere that you should always stay with your boat when you are in trouble. I reasoned that if my boat were to wreck, I would try to steer to a sandy beach to land on instead of rocks and cliffs. Then I could just step off and walk the rest of the way to the shore.

Thankfully, I made it to the lee side of Maury Island. The wind wasn't as bad on the lee side of the island, so I felt more hopeful about making it back in one piece. The wind finally abated as I rounded Brown's point. As my boat limped down Foss Harbor and neared the marina with the jib sail wrapped around the shrouds, my neighbors who lived in a catamaran on the outside of a pier at the marina waved at me. Later, they questioned me about the sorry state of my boat, and I told them the story. Any trip you return from is a good one!

I learned a lot from that trip. It made the next windstorm much easier to handle. I made some changes to the boat. I re-mounted the VHF radio near the top of the hatch so I could reach it while handling the tiller. I remounted the mainsail traveler and secured it with hefty stainless-steel bolts to stop the car from sliding off. Now, when routing the jib sheets, I put a knot in the line after threading it through the pulleys, so the lines don't end up in the water. I learned how to reef the mainsail so it wouldn't catch so much wind during storms. Now, when entering a hard blowing wind, I make sure the mainsail is at a 180-degree angle to it. Then I will gradually pull the mainsail in from the blocks. As the boat's speed increases, I will start turning downwind while easing up on the mainsail. A lot of times when a strong wind is blowing in the direction I'm headed and I'm sailing single handed, I will only put up the jib and not the mainsail. Indeed, the next storm wasn't nearly as scary. Probably the most important thing I learned was having the experience itself. The way I prioritized and handled the problems one at a time built up my confidence.

CHAPTER 27: DON'T BE "THAT SAILOR"

When sailing or cruising your boat on Puget Sound, you will encounter other boat traffic. There are commercial cargo ships, barge traffic, sailboats, kayaks, and motorized craft. Some new sailors get the idea that boats under sail always have the right of way over boats under power. I implore you to read and learn the "Rules of the Road". They are contained in COLREGS, which is the "International Regulations for Preventing Collisions at Sea" handbook. Boats over a certain length require this book to be on board, and Coast Guard inspectors like to see this book on your shelf. This book contains an international standard of rules published to increase safety while navigating bodies of water. In its rules, there is a whole hierarchy of vessels that are given consideration for the right of way. You should read these regulations and keep a copy on your boat for reference. Even though you may have the right of way in a certain situation, don't push the issue. I have heard anecdotes of cargo ships reaching their destination, only to find a sailboat stuck on their prow. One day while I was cruising along, I heard a one-sided conversation over the marine VHF radio on channel 16. A very frustrated barge captain was fuming at a sailboat's pilot, "I can't turn!", he said, "You are the kind of people that give sail boaters a bad name!", he cursed. When you're out there with your sailboat, don't be that skipper! COLREGS also states that navigators should do everything in their power to avoid collisions. Collisions occur more often than you might think, usually because one or both captains did not apply the Rules of the Road.

CHAPTER 28: THE IMPORTANCE OF KEEPING IN SHAPE

At retirement age, I feel fortunate to have the physical strength and endurance to sail. Over the years, even though I had a sedentary desk job, I kept physically active. I commuted to work on my bicycle, took long walks and hikes, and went to the gym regularly to swim and work out. I recently added Tai Chi and Qigong workouts to keep limber. Even though my new lifestyle while living aboard forces me to perform physical labor, kayak and walk a lot while carrying heavy objects, sailing can still be hard work. After the first few sailing trips at the beginning of the season, it can take me a day or two to recover. If you are young and hale, you will recuperate more quickly, but it's always a good idea to exercise and warm up before sailing. You will have more fun and be a better sailor if you can perform strenuous activities. Did I mention swimming? It could save your or someone else's life. There will be a time when I won't be able to sail singlehandedly. As I get older, I will bring more crew aboard, and teach them to sail. They will help me sail and carry on the legacy of the Seattle Singles Yacht Club founding members.

CHAPTER 29:
CAMPING ON A BOAT

This section contains observations, ruminations, and some conclusions I made over the past few years. Most of the time I am on the water, it is so quiet, I can hear the current flowing and the wavelets lapping against the hull. I can see perturbations, standing vibrations in the reflection of the water, long before I hear or see a power boat approaching. I can also see these disturbances in the waves when a loud airplane or helicopter is overhead. You have a lot of time to notice things when you are sailing. Sound waves travel faster in water than they do in the air. I think about how this must affect whales, dolphins, and other sea mammals. They find their food by echolocation and talk to each other by making their sounds under water. Boaters are recommended to set their fish finders to 200khz or turn them off to avoid interfering with their hunting: "In areas where Southern Residents may be present, setting depth finders to 200 kHz frequency or temporarily turning them off. Underwater transducers, such as depth finders, can overlap with echolocation frequencies that Southern Resident killer whales use to find food, communicate, and travel through Washington's waters.". You can find more information on protecting Orcas at https://wdfw.wa.gov/species-habitats/at-risk/species-recovery/orca. I can only imagine how much noise interferes with sea mammals' lives. It is one reason why the resident Puget Sound Orcas are endangered. I have read that loud noises under water can make whales panic. They will expend a lot of energy swimming several miles away from the source of the noise before they can relax and continue with their lives. Loud undersea noise can also be the cause of mass stranding events on beaches.

Camping on the water is incomparable with camping on land. Simply driving to a camping spot and setting up your tent isn't getting away from it all. Sure, instead of being surrounded by houses, presumably there are trees, trails, and maybe a body of water nearby. I thought camping at a Washington Marine State Park while tied up to a mooring ball or at anchor in a quiet cove would be getting away from it all. But it wasn't desolate or pristine. Everywhere you go on Puget Sound, there are always signs of civilization.

As I spent more time on the water, I found that every week or two, I needed to refill the water tank with potable water for drinking and washing, empty the sewage holding tank, and take out the trash. When I was docked at my home port, I could go to a big box store and stock up on canned goods. For perishable items, I would go to local grocers. If I was lucky, I would find a farmer's market near my anchorage. I would buy fruit and vegetables that would either keep well, or that I could eat quickly before they spoiled. At the beginning of a trip, I would cook and eat all the healthy, delicious foods like grilled fish tacos with mango salsa and cilantro. As the days passed on the water, I would make interesting use of the canned foods that remained. Apples, oranges, and mangos kept well, as would onions, garlic, and sweet potatoes. I love bananas, but they need to be eaten in a few days. I kept the fruit and vegetables in hanging colanders to keep some air flow around them. They keep from molding that way. I sometimes noticed fruit flies, and I would spend a few moments persuading them to go outside. They didn't eat much, so I justified their existence as my pets. If the flies got too annoying, I would put the fruit in my full-sized ice chest. I kept healthy by eating foods that fulfilled my nutrient requirements.

I took a stab at foraging, living off nature's bounty by fishing and picking berries whenever I could. I even bought a fishing license, a net without knots to release fish unharmed back into the water, and descending rigs used to return deep water fish quickly to the bottom, so they had a better chance of survival. Rules, regulations, and requirements for fishing in Washington are listed on the Washington Department of Fish and Wildlife (WDFW) web site at wdfw.wa.gov. I did catch some keepers, small flounder, and rockfish, but I felt sorry for them and released them. In the zones used by the Washington Department of Fish and Wildlife that I travelled in, I could set crab traps 2 days of the week. I love Dungeness crab but didn't catch any keepers. All the ports and towns I visited around Puget Sound had permanent signs posted prohibiting the harvesting of shellfish due to pollution or bacterial contamination. Although I did see some people digging for clams in these areas. If you plan to forage for survival, it will take some research to comply with regulations and techniques. There are certain times of the year when squid and Coho salmon travel through the Puget Sound area when you could survive on what you caught. I will read more on harvesting seafood and get the help of more experienced people as time goes on. Many kinds of seaweed are edible, but I need to do more research on them. I do buy seaweed snacks and add them to soups. But for now, I plan to get the food I need from farmer's markets, small butcher shops, and big box stores. It bothers me that the First People nations had managed this land and harvested it responsibly for thousands of years, but it only took a few hundred years for Europeans to come to this country and destroy this natural cornucopia.

Another constraint is the amount of water my boat can carry. It has two 15-gallon water tanks. The tanks and a few gallons of bottled water would last me more than 2 weeks. Out of curiosity, I looked up per capita water use for the U.S. It is 85 gallons per day! In contrast, my water consumption was less than 4 gallons per day.

Mold and Mildew – the Fungus Among Us

Mold will find any excuse to grow. It will grow on cloth or

other porous surfaces in damp areas with little air circulation. I had some mold problems during the first winter, mainly because I had removed the thin layer of insulation from inside the hull. Even though I used a bleach solution to kill it and bought a dehumidifier to reduce humidity in my boat, the mold still grew back. I read some tips from a Foss Harbor Marina pamphlet regarding non-toxic options for keeping your boat clean. Vinegar, lemon juice, and baking soda are safer to use, both for you and the marine life around your boat. I read that mold can survive bleach; however, they will happily drink vinegar and die from the mild acetic acid in it. The best way to keep mold from growing is to keep the interior of your boat dry, insulating the hull, and ensuring all areas have ventilation. After sealing all the nagging little leaks from the windows and deck and insulating the hull, I taped bubble wrap around the windows and frames to prevent drips from condensation from forming on the cold bronze frames. Mold loves to grow on cloth items laid up against the walls. I made the mattress for my berth by cutting up the memory foam mattress I kept when moving out of my house. By using the curved slats from the bed, air was able to circulate under the mattress. However, one time I discovered mold growing between the mattress where it met the insulated hull. After cleaning the Naugahyde with vinegar, I put an air gap between the bedding and the hull, and the mold never came back. The galley has a special vent that lets air in but keeps rain and spray from the ocean out. To improve ventilation and to pull odors out of the head, I cut a hole in the bathroom ceiling and installed a continuously operating solar powered marine fan. This would provide cross ventilation, keeping air circulating throughout the cabin. After taking these precautions, I have yet to find any mold. I didn't need the dehumidifier anymore, so I sold it at a garage sale.

The Head

The bathroom on boats is called the "head". I wondered why it was called that. From what I read, the toilets on ships were put in the bow where the waves would break and carry the waste away. Nowadays we have inside plumbing on boats and holding tanks for the waste that you need to pump out occasionally. Many marinas have free pump out facilities. In Washington, there is a cellphone app to find the closest one. There are pump out boats that will come to you if you don't want to leave your anchorage. When I bought the boat, I installed a new Jabsco toilet, but after having to replace the joker valve every few months, I bought a Raritan unit. A joker valve is made of soft rubber that allows material to flow through it one way, but not the other way. They can deteriorate over time or be blocked open by sediment or other objects. You can tell if you need a joker valve when flushed stuff doesn't stay flushed. Replacing a joker valve is probably the worst thing that will ever happen to you. If I end up going to hell, I will spend eternity replacing joker valves. The Raritan toilet is very reliable. After 3 years, I finally had to replace the original valve. Replacing the head saved me around 12 times I didn't have to replace the joker valve. I can live with that.

Gravity

One thing I learned in the early days of living on my boat was to not leave anything such as screws, food on a plate, or beverages without lids, unattended. Boats tend to roll, thus changing the vector of the force of gravity acting on a container and causing objects to fall and break or scatter on the floor. I have cleaned up many spills and broken glass from items deemed safe on a countertop or table.

Wake and Smell the Coffee

I rely on coffee to start my day. Even if I shed all other accoutrements of civilization, I must still have coffee. While at dock, I had a routine of preparing the coffee maker for the next day. It was a simple 4 cup drip machine with a glass carafe. Every night before retiring, I filled the reservoir with water, place the filter and add a couple of tablespoons of ground coffee. One night while anchored in Kingston Harbor, I woke to the boat rolling violently and heard things hitting the floor. Apparently, a ferry had taken the corner into the harbor too hot, raising a huge wake. After my boat settled down, I gingerly made my way down the companionway. There, I found the coffee grounds mixed with water on the floor. Fortunately, the glass carafe didn't break! So, now when moored anywhere other than my marina, I wait until morning before filling the coffee pot.

Metal's Affinity for Water

When working on projects on your boat's exterior, be sure to secure your tools so they don't fall in. Water attracts the metal in your tools. I also believe, from the number of tools I have dropped overboard, that gravity is stronger over water. I use light-duty paracord to tie my tools and secure them with a carabiner clip attached to my belt. I also have a heavy-duty magnet tied to a rope to retrieve steel objects that have fallen overboard. The magnet came with the boat. Although it is time consuming, I have been able to successfully retrieve about half of the things I've dropped into the drink. The largest object being my electric scooter. I used it to travel back and forth from my boat to the marina office or my car. I normally parked the scooter on top of my storage box on the pier, but one day, I leaned it up against the side of my boat with the handlebar inside the hull inside the scuppers. I would only take a second to retrieve an item I left in the boat. My pier was well away from the channel, and because there was a "no wake" sign in the harbor, my boat didn't move around much. But occasionally, someone would go too fast down the Foss Harbor channel and raise a wake. My neighbors would yell at boats that were going too fast, "SLOW DOWN!". My scooter fell into the water between my boat and the pier. I brought out the magnet and fished it out, but the damage was done. The lithium batteries shorted out in the salt water and had caught on fire. Luckily, the scooter was one of the low powered machines that had problems climbing the slightest slope. I took the batteries to be recycled and threw the frame away. Don't lean anything against the side of your boat and expect it to stay there. It only takes a moment for things to go wrong on the water.

Showering at Marinas

I don't have a hot-water shower in my boat yet. I decided to swim, take sponge baths, or shower at the marinas. I had a solar hot water heater in a bag. When camping, you could hang this bag on a tree branch in the sun and enjoy a shower at the end of the day. Although the bag had scalding temperature warnings printed on it, it didn't even get lukewarm while on my boat. I think I found out why the water didn't get very warm. I laid it in the scuppers with the clear side up and the black side down. On a tree, the bag was insulated by the air, but on the boat, the solid, cool fiberglass drew the heat away from it. Next summer, I will put a piece of foam under it to insulate the bag from the deck. Restrooms and shower facilities at marinas run the gamut. While some of them are spacious, well-ventilated, and clean, there are others that are dank and mildewy with filthy floors. The Kingston marina has free, clean showers. Although Poulsbo Marina has large, modern, and clean restrooms, with 3 shower stalls in the men's room, the showers require quarters. 25 cents will buy you 5 minutes. I have been to other marina showers where I don't even want to take off my clothes and shoes. Such is the case at West Bay Marina. Although free, the 2 showers in the men's room are out of order. They are closed off and appear to be in the process of being remodeled, although I have never seen anyone working on them. I don't know what is available in the women's room. There is a single unisex handicapped shower available. As you walk into it, you will find muddy water on the floor with a half wall partition separating the shower from the dressing area. Apparently, water can enter the dressing area if you stand too close to the shower head. You will also see a long-handled tool the size of a janitor's push broom, but with squeegees instead of broom bristles. After you remove the hair from the shower drain, you use this tool to scrape the water and mud out of the dressing area. Then you can take your shower. Afterwards, while dressing, putting your socks and shoes on is problematic. I have found that folding your towel in half and placing it over the mud puddle in the dressing area works OK, if you put your underwear and pants on first. Then, after rolling your pant legs up, keep one foot elevated while putting on the sock and shoe, then repeat the process with the other foot. My Tai Chi and Ninjitsu training is very helpful with this. I really should buy some flipflops or rubber shoes. It is a miracle I don't have athlete's foot fungus by now!

CHAPTER 30: CONSTRAINTS OF LIVING ON A SOLAR POWERED OFF-THE-GRID SAILBOAT

Summer in the Pacific Northwest is perfect. The weather is always warm and dry with hardly a cloud in the sky. The temperature rarely gets above 80 degrees. Daylight seems to last forever. During this time of year, my solar array puts out 1200 watts of power. I have measured the current from the panels at 7 amps, and the batteries were always topped off. When I started this project, I had a set of four 12-volt AGM deep cycle batteries hooked up in parallel and an inverter to run my refrigerator, microwave, DVD player, stereo, and 32" monitor. I had another set of AGM deep cycle 12-volt batteries wired in series to produce 48 volts for the inboard electric motor. I figured I could stay at anchor forever until the sun fully recharged the storage batteries. As I ventured out for longer distance trips and stayed out for weeks at a time, I realized that I didn't have enough battery storage. It seemed that most of the time the wind would blow counter to my planned direction of travel. People asked me if I considered using lithium batteries for the drive batteries. In the planning stage of this project, I did. After a lot of research, I decided not to go with lithium technology. I would have had to invest at least 5 times more money in 48v batteries, lithium battery chargers, and design a fire suppressant system. I couldn't use the more economical 12-volt lithium batteries, because their built-in BMS (battery management systems) prohibited wiring those batteries in series to achieve 48 volts required to run the boat motor. At the time when I was planning the electricity storage system, there was a news story about a cargo ship with millions of dollars' worth of exotic sport cars catching on fire off the coast of Europe. It was apparently caused by a crew member using the wrong type of charger for one of the electric cars on board. I can't imagine anything more terrifying than a fire on your boat when you are miles away from the shore. So, I bought two more sets of four AGM batteries, one group 31 with 120 amp-hours and another set of 200 amp-hour batteries from Renogy. These gave me a cruising range of up to 60 miles depending on wind and currents.

While on the water, as the autumn days grew shorter and cloudier, I began using more electricity than my solar panels were generating. I had to monitor the batteries daily. If the batteries dropped below 11 volts, they could be ruined. Fortunately, the solar power controllers and inverters will sound an alarm before this occurs. I calculated the power draw for the appliances and ranked them in order of necessity. I needed enough power to run the radio, lights, navigation system, cell phone and laptop, but they didn't draw much current. The inverter used some power to convert the DC to AC to run the household appliances, but the real power hogs were the refrigerator, microwave oven, the coffee maker, and the stereo with powered speakers. I used the microwave oven a lot during the summer. I found that it could be used to cook almost anything. Shrimp in the microwave is surprisingly good. Although I used propane for the barbeque grill, I resisted using the propane heater or the gas stove. The propane system is safe enough. It uses a solenoid to turn on the gas flow from the tank located in a properly ventilated compartment to the rear of the cockpit. There were several carbon monoxide and smoke detectors in the cabin and the engine compartment. Although it would be safe to use propane, I just didn't like using fossil fuels at all. One cold and blustery fall day, I succumbed to using the gas stove. It was so nice to be warm and eat hot food again. I had insulated the cabin well; I didn't need to use the gas heater at night while I was sleeping. It would stay warm enough if I preheated the cabin and then turned off the gas. Besides, an electric mattress pad kept me warm enough to sleep, and it didn't take much electricity. I relinquished the use of the entertainment center but was able to watch video on the laptop. I made it a point to download video and music whenever I had Wi-Fi internet. On my trips, I would occasionally pay for moorage with shore power just to charge the batteries up. I knew when I adopted this lifestyle there would be some constraints. Next summer I will add some more electricity generation to my boat. As for now, I am surviving nicely with what I have.

Conserving Electricity While Navigating

When motoring my 30' sailboat, I am always mindful of how much energy I'm using. I have a digital ammeter ring on my motor's positive cable that shows my energy consumption. Using it, regardless of current and wind vectors, I can optimize the boat's speed to get the most out of my battery banks.

Garbage Tips

On a weeklong journey, the food scraps you throw away will begin to decompose, smell, and attract fruit flies. If I am near a marina or town that has a community garden, I donate my vegetable peels to their compost pile or worm bin. Otherwise, I use the fruit and vegetable bags from the grocery store to bag food scraps and put them in the 13-gallon plastic garbage can in the head (bathroom). One of my first projects was to cut a hole in the head's ceiling and install a solar exhaust fan. The Marinco fan runs constantly and keeps smells from entering the cabin. It also keeps air circulating around the cabin to keep mold from growing. Don't throw your food scraps overboard. It's against the law. There are 3 placards you need to post inside your boat to pass the Coast Guard inspection. One of them says to not throw garbage into the water. If your boat is of a certain size, you need to have a formal plan for disposing of your garbage. The other 2 rules are "don't spill your fuel into the water" and "don't pump your sewage into the water". You can find these placards at marine stores or on the Internet.

CHAPTER 31:
NOTES ON SAILS
AND RIGGING

You may be tempted to buy new sails for your used boat right away. Unless your sails are in tatters, don't. It's better to learn how your boat handles using the sails it came with. Then you can improve on what you have. The mainsail that came with my boat needed to be replaced. I worked with the sail manufacturer's team. They sent me forms and instructions on how to measure the mast position and height, the boom length and height, and the type of clips and fasteners used to secure the sail. For some reason, maybe because the sailcloth being used was named "Bainbridge HSX", after the island in Washington, I thought the sails were manufactured in the US or Canada. They were designed in Vancouver, Canada, but were manufactured in China and flown back to a distribution center in North America. The new sail was made with the latest sailcloth and design techniques. It was of good quality and fit well, and delivered about four weeks after I submitted the measurements. I was pleased with the turnaround time, and the new mainsail worked well. It was bright white with a black Rawson logo on it, "3R". However, it made the jib sail look old and decrepit. The old jib sail had a few patches, was kind of baggy and dragged on the deck. I don't even think it was made for this boat but salvaged from another boat. Since my previous experience went well, I selected the same manufacturer to build a new jib sail. I made the measurements and worked with a designer who recommended a 115% jib sail. The measurements were quite different than my original sail. The clew corner of the sail was 5 feet off the deck and 15% of the sail extended aft of the mast. I waited almost 2 months for the new sail to arrive. After sailing a few times under varying conditions, I found the new jib sail was useless when the wind was coming from behind the boat. It only filled out and contributed when close-hauled or on a beam reach, that is the wind was almost perpendicular to the boat's direction of travel. With both sails up, the force of the wind pushed too far aft of the center of the boat, making balancing almost impossible. When your sails are balanced, you don't have to keep a lot of force on the tiller or wheel to keep going straight. If you must keep force on the tiller, its friction with the water slows the boat down. The new jib sail ended up being a disappointment. In retrospect, I should have ordered a smaller jib sail that didn't extend past the mast. It would have been a lot more useful and easier to tack with. Sails last for a long time if kept out of the sun, so I will have to wait a while before justifying the expenditure for a replacement jib sail. I might try cutting the sail and sewing it myself, but I would need access to a heavy duty, industrial sewing machine. So, if your current sails are serviceable, I highly recommend sailing with them until you learn how your boat handles. Then, you will be in a better position to determine the new sails' measurements. Because of Seattle's mild summer breezes, and my sail manufacturers were having a 20% off sale, I also bought a 150 Genoa. It worked well for those extremely light winds. I also have a storm jib that came with the boat. It is small and fits well. If I am sailing single handedly and know there will be high winds, I will start off with the storm jib. If I had to do the sails all over again, I would hire a professional to recommend the measurements and types of new sails.

While we are on the topic of sails; because I sail alone most of the time, it was difficult and time consuming to get the new mainsail to fold neatly over the boom and wrap the sail cover over it. Especially when coming back into port and there were a million other things to do quickly. New sails are very stiff, like a new shirt that has been starched and ironed. I had seen a lazy jack on other sailboats, which was a system of ropes and pullies designed to hold the mainsail as it was dropped. I examined several on the boats near me, then looked for them online. They seemed expensive for what they were. So, I made some measurements, and drew a plan. Then I bought some nylon rope, heavy duty paracord and blue marine canvas and made my own. I used some of the knots I learned and strung the ropes from the aft shrouds, and sewed two sail covers. One was for the boom to hold the sail as it dropped, and one was for the top to protect the sail from the sun. Needless exposure to the sun greatly reduces the life of a sail. My system required a little adjustment at first but works great now. I can drop the mainsail in an instant and not worry about it falling all over the place and getting in my way while racing around the deck.

Rigging is what keeps your mast from breaking and falling into the water when there is a lot of stress from the sails. While there are articles on how to adjust the rigging yourself, I recommend hiring a professional rigger to tune your rigging, at least for the first time. The mast has fore and aft stays. The stays on the sides are called shrouds. The stays are attached to chainplates imbedded into the hull. A sailor friend of mine suggests that the chainplates should be imbedded as deep and secure as possible. One last thing, you can recycle old sails by sending them to a company called Sea Bags. They will let you pick out one of their new bags in exchange. Here is the link: https://seabags.com/our-company/sea-bags-sail-trade-program.html.

CHAPTER 32: THE DARK SIDE

Sometimes I hear the phrase "I went to the dark side" uttered during my yacht club meetings. This means that someone sold or traded their sailboat to buy a motorboat or cabin cruiser. Skippers make this choice for several reasons. As sailors get older, they still love being on the water, but feel that they aren't strong or agile enough to sail. Maybe they have time constraints and want to get to different locations around the water faster. Or maybe they won the lottery. Cabin cruisers are made to entertain. When a cabin cruiser backs up to the dock, the wide stern and gate in the back gives an easy entrance onto the boat. They are like mobile, floating living rooms with large windows, sliding glass doors, and a patio. The galley (kitchen) area can be very luxurious with modern up-to-date finishes, stainless steel refrigerators and stoves with convection ovens. Not to mention staterooms (bedrooms) with heads (bathrooms). Cabin cruisers have all the electronic equipment for navigation and large, powerful gasoline or diesel engines. A cabin cruiser can have multiple engines with 600 horsepower or more and achieve speeds of 50 knots or more. Their fuel consumption is measured in gallons per hour. For example, one new cabin cruiser had a top speed of 47 knots (54.6 mph), with its two 600 horsepower engines gulping over 60 gallons per hour. I see a lot of cabin cruisers on Lake Union. You don't have to use a lot of fuel while idling around the lake, and there are good restaurants on the shore. Sailboats can also be luxurious with nearly the same capacity for entertainment, but you will pay more because your boat has all the additional equipment for sailing. And, unless the sailing yacht is very large, it will not have those huge windows or sliding glass doors. They just aren't practical. The strength of waves in bad weather can shatter those huge windows. Engines for sailboats are generally a fraction of the size required for cabin cruisers. Sailboats have displacement hulls that are designed to be efficient. My 30' Rawson sailboat has a 10-kilowatt electric motor, equivalent to 13 horsepower. A displacement hull's top speed is limited by the length of the boat at the waterline. The mathematical formula for this is 1.34 times the square root of the vessel's length. For my boat, the hull speed is 6.3 knots, or about 7 miles per hour. As quoted from Wikipedia, "Hull speed or displacement speed is the speed at which the wavelength of a vessel's bow wave is equal to the waterline length of the vessel. As boat speed increases from rest, the wavelength of the bow wave increases, and usually its crest-to-trough dimension (height) increases as well. When hull speed is exceeded, a vessel in displacement mode will appear to be climbing up the back of its bow wave.". Although a boat with a displacement hull can go faster than hull speed, it requires much more power to climb the bow wave.

Although the hull speed of my boat is around 6.3 knots, I have found the most efficient speed for my boat, given the constraints of its 13-horsepower electric motor and batteries, is about 4 knots. Occasionally, I will be passed by a good-sized cabin cruiser going 30 knots, often within 50 to 100 feet, even though we are in the middle of a large bay, with its deafening twin 600hp engines swilling gallons of fuel every hour. It seems that much of the power of boats like that is spent climbing the bow wave instead of pushing the boat forward. This makes a wake so high that I am forced to alter course and turn my boat into it to avoid being swamped or rolled. Well, at least you can hear them coming. Which brings me back to the "dark side" quote.

Imagine, if you will, a beautiful day with bright sunshine, blue sky, and sparkling water, and a sailboat catching the wind with outspread sails. Then imagine the same day with yellow-grey smoke laden air, an oil refinery in the background, and dull water reflecting a rainbow sheen from the fuel spilled on it. We can even throw in a few dead fish, or a dead, bloated seal, or whale with oozing sores on its back from being hit with a ship's propeller, to complete the picture. Then you will understand the full impact of "going to the dark side".

CHAPTER 33: ORCAS

I saw Orcas in the wild for the first time on the Bremerton to Seattle ferry, while commuting to work. The captain stopped the engines and announced that a pod of Orcas was nearby. As the ferry coasted silently through the water, everybody went to the windows and rails and searched the water for them. I saw shadows glide ghostly by, two or three of them. "There they are", someone whispered. Most people have reverence and awe for them. I don't think anyone minded the delay while on their way to work!

One day while sailing south from Jarrell Cove State Park, I saw what looked like a log in the water with birds standing on it. I took the binoculars out and realized the "birds" were Orca whales. I had never been this close to Orcas before. One of them had a dorsal fin that looked like "Free Willy's". I saw that they were feeding on something, probably a seal or sea lion. There is a law in Washington prohibiting boats from approaching the Southern Resident Orcas. It occurred to me that these weren't the Southern Resident Orcas that live in Puget Sound and only eat salmon, but transient Orcas visiting from some other place. I wasn't going to ask them what pod they belonged to, so I turned and slowly headed away from them. I made sure I was well away from them before resuming my course to the south. I also turned off my depth finder so it wouldn't interfere with the Orcas' echolocation. I had heard of Orcas biting the rudders off or sinking sailboats in the Atlantic Ocean off the coasts of Spain and Portugal. One theory behind those incidents was an Orca had been injured by a propeller, and they taught each other to attack the rudders as revenge. I haven't heard of similar

Orca behavior in Puget Sound, yet. Then, I heard a power boat coming. It appeared to be headed straight for the pod, how close I didn't know as I was much further away. I heard the boat slow down momentarily, and I heard a shout ring out as it neared the whales, but then it sped up almost immediately. I can only imagine what passed through the minds of those boaters, but in my opinion, they were too close. Next time I see Orcas, I will raise the whale flag that I picked up from an environmental booth at a boat show in Seattle. There are state laws in Washington to protect the Resident Orcas, but strangely, not the transient Orca population. Here is the law:

"... At minimum, giving Southern Residents at least 300 yards on either side and 400 yards in front of and behind them. Avoid approaching Southern Resident killer whales within 1,000 yards. Legislation passed in 2023 increases the mandatory distance to 1,000 yards beginning in 2025.

Reducing their speed to seven knots within one-half nautical mile of Southern Residents.

In areas where Southern Residents may be present, setting depth finders to 200 kHz frequency or temporarily turning them off. Underwater transducers, such as depth finders, can overlap with echolocation frequencies that Southern Resident killer whales use to find food, communicate, and travel through Washington's waters.

Watching for the Whale Warning Flag, an optional tool from the San Juan County Marine Resources Committee that lets others know that there are whales nearby. If boaters see the flag, they should slow down and continue to follow Be Whale Wise regulations and guidelines."

CHAPTER 34:
NOISE AND THE
ENVIRONMENT

I read an article in the Sunday, December 31, 2023, edition of the New York Times. It said that "Research suggests noise from shipping, oil exploration and other underwater human activities may make it harder for dolphins to communicate and work together". I believe this is true. If I can hear power boats approaching from miles away, how much louder is this for our underwater cousins who use their voices to coordinate activities and echolocation to find their food? Especially since sound travels much further and faster through water. One day as I was sailing around Commencement Bay outside of Tacoma, I saw a humpback whale breach high out of the water and perform a belly flop. I will never forget the sight of that magnificent creature and how big it appeared compared to the fleet of small fishing boats near it. Later, I wondered if it was bothered by the noise of the fishing boats and their fish finders. I recently read articles about whale songs. Baleen whales have a special voice box that enables them to sing underwater by recycling air in their lungs. The common element I read in these articles is how human made noise in the ocean is disrupting whales feeding, mating, and survival. Scientists have tracked whales swimming frantically for hours away from submarine and ship sonar, and blasting used for sea floor mapping. The whales were panicking. Sometimes, it's human made noise that causes mass whale stranding events. Whales and other sea mammals aren't stupid. Hungry Orca whales have learned how to steal tuna from the long lines fishing boats use. Other Orcas have learned how to disable boats by tearing their rudders off. One theory is that an adult Orca was hit by a propeller, so she is teaching the others to exact their revenge on boats. Neuroscientist Lori Marino, president of the Whale Sanctuary Project says that "Humans cannot even be expected to imagine how killer whales experience the world. They don't just see the world, they hear it, echolocating and building a picture of their world based on a stream of visual and acoustic information that is all processed at the same time." "And their ability to process information is orders of magnitude faster than ours," she says. "If you look at how they respond to one another when they're in a pod or a group - there's a seamlessness to their interaction." In other words, they can be in sync in ways that our own brains are not wired to fathom. Here are the links for the articles I've read.

Whale song mystery solved by scientists: https://www.bbc.com/news/science-environment-68358414.

Atlantic orcas 'learning from adults' to target boats: https://www.bbc.com/news/science-environment-66384045.

First direct measurements of behavioural responses by Cuvier's beaked whales to mid-frequency active sonar: https://royalsocietypublishing.org/doi/full/10.1098/rsbl.2013.0223

Noise: https://www.bbc.com/news/science-environment-56676820.

Orcas are smart: https://www.bbc.co.uk/news/extra/buqvasp1rr/orcas-spain-portugal.

The Whale Sanctuary Project: https://whalesanctuaryproject.org.

CHAPTER 35: AIRPLANES, HELICOPTERS, AND JETS

While living aboard my boat at Foss Harbor Marina, from time to time I heard police helicopters flying around, evidently looking for perpetrators. Sometimes I would hear the big twin rotor cargo helicopters overhead, perhaps on a journey to deliver things from one military base to another. Sometimes I would hear cargo planes or passenger jets. Other times, I would hear the buzz of private planes. I thought the aircraft noise would diminish and it would be quieter as I travelled further away from civilization. But it didn't and wasn't. It occurred to me that aircraft tended to fly across water to shield the noise from people in the cities. Maybe there will be a utopian society many years from now, where people aren't using fossil fuels to get from one place to another in a hurry, when you may see dirigibles ghosting through the air and sailboats making their way across oceans, where the quality of life and talking with the people around you is more important than what you own or how fast you go.

CHAPTER 36: LIVEABOARD COMMUNITY

In my opinion, there is an opportunity to promote aquatic communities, and revisit the rules and laws that were made to restrict the number of people who are allowed to live aboard their boats at marinas. These rules were made to regulate shoreline usage and development and to protect the environment. Since there are laws prohibiting pumping sewage into the Puget Sound and pump out facilities are conveniently found at most of the marinas, state parks, and city docks, rules could be changed to allow higher density of live aboard boats in marinas. The current state rule permits marinas to designate 10% of their slips as liveaboards, although this can be overridden at the local government level. Marinas can charge a premium for liveaboard occupancy to cover expenses for maintenance due to increased use of marina facilities. Many marinas that allow liveaboards provide a weekly pump out service for their tenants.

There are quite a few benefits of allowing people to live aboard their vessels. They become a community who cares about their neighborhood. We greet and chat with our neighbors, and we all have something in common, our love of boating! Marinas and yacht clubs provide facilities like tenants' lounges and meeting halls, where tenants host cookouts, movie nights, and dances. At one of the marinas I lived at, we even invited people walking along the esplanade to join our parties. This had the effect of building an authentic community, not just for the boaters, but also for our neighbors who live nearby. We discuss life near the water and trade information on how to reduce incidences of theft or vandalism in the area. Residents are on hand to notify marina staff or emergency services when there are problems on the docks, such as fires or sinking boats. I lived in Foss Harbor Marina for several years. It is not in the best of neighborhoods. But, while there were hundreds of thefts in parking lots around the area, there were only 2 incidences that occurred inside the marina's gates.

Residential Aquatic Land Use Rules

By rule, Washington State Department of Natural Resources allows the residential use of aquatic lands by vessels and floating homes subject to certain restrictions. In general, residential use is limited to 10 percent of the slips in a marina unless the local government adopts another. The rules are different between floating houses and vessels that can be lived in. Here are some relevant links for liveaboard rules in Washington:
U of W liveaboard article: https://sites.uw.edu/curreri/2013/08/16/live-on-a-boat/
Port of Seattle liveaboard Information: https://www.portseattle.org/page/liveaboard-information
Shilshole Marina Liveaboard Association: https://shilsholecommunity.org/
Port of Friday Harbor Live-aboard Policy: https://mrsc.org/getmedia/a21051bc-f286-4cc2-8b3c-0c39985d9308/s77p6fhLiveaboardPol.pdf.aspx

CHAPTER 37:
LIVEABOARD LIFE

"Living on a boat has long been a fantasy for many in the Pacific Northwest. It offers the chance to escape hectic city living and exchange it for hectic water living. " Evan Bush, Seattle Times, May 14, 2018. A compelling title for the article, but I disagree about the hectic living part. I am in my 4th year of living aboard my 30-foot sailboat. Living aboard can be uncomfortable or stressful at times. However, if you plan your life around the conditions on the water, realize that your resources will be more limited, and accept the extra work it takes, this is not a hectic life. Since the pandemic, many people continue to work remotely. Satellite Internet is pervasive and getting cheaper all the time. I have felt more relaxed and safer knowing there is a buffer of water separating me from crime on land. I kept my van for the times I must drive, however, from nearly every port you travel to by boat, you can ride public transportation to any other city around the Sound. Many of the busses are cheap or even free. Plus, any public transportation around Puget Sound can be paid for by using the ORCA card. The cost of a marina slip is much less than what one would pay for land-based housing, with its rent or mortgage payments, homeowner association dues, utilities, insurance, and taxes. You use less energy because your living space is smaller, better insulated, and less drafty. All the furniture on your boat is built in. You will declutter your life. While there is usually enough space for you to have boating equipment, life jackets, tools, food and clothing, there's not a lot of extra space to fill up with stuff.

Because of miniaturization and technology, you can get good quality video and sound by downloading them to your laptop. I didn't get satellite internet yet, mainly because of the power drain it takes to keep the dish pointed at the right spot and for signal amplification. So, whenever I get free Wi-Fi, I take the opportunity to download new video and MP3 music tracks. I live in a 30-foot sailboat, and the amount of interior room is about the same size as a walk-in closet, yet I have a nice entertainment center with waterproof Bluetooth speakers and a 32" TV monitor. I have a 10-million-dollar view of the water and nature all around me. If I grow tired of my view or neighborhood, I can cruise around until I find another one. For myself, I would rather pay for boat maintenance than all the expenses of a house. Living on a boat gives you a great sense of freedom that you can't find while permanently anchored in a house.

I hope that this book will encourage you to learn how to sail, consider replacing your sailboat's gas or diesel engine with an electric motor, or to try the marine lifestyle. I realize that there may be other factors in your life that would make this dream impossible for now; hopefully you will keep these ideas in mind until you are able to act on them. In the marina or at sea, I have met young people, retirees, even families with young children living on boats here on Puget Sound. There are civilizations whose people have lived on their boats on the waterways around the world for centuries. This is hardly a new idea. These peoples are the explorers who find and settle new lands around the world.

CHAPTER 38: SOLAR ROOFS VS. SOLAR FARMS

I have recently read articles comparing the benefits of solar electricity on rooftops versus large scale solar installations. These articles favor individual rooftop solar electricity generation because there is much less power wasted in electricity lost in transmission lines. Solar installations built on rooftops can also be cheaper because they don't need much mounting infrastructure. They also don't take up space on vacant land which could be used for farming or better purposes. There are a few parking lots with solar roofs sheltering the cars underneath, which can be further enhanced with charging stations for electric cars. I have seen many more parking lots that could easily support solar panels. Homeowners that have their own electricity generation and storage would avoid power outages due to storms and power grid problems. Rooftop solar would be a lifesaver for those who depend on air conditioning or require uninterrupted electricity to power medical devices. Although at this time I can't generate all the electricity I need during the winter with its short days in the cloudy Pacific Northwest, I can keep my batteries topped off and would survive nicely for several weeks until power is restored. I just might talk to my marina's management and mention selling my excess electricity to the grid. Electricity from solar installations is now cheaper than that from conventional coal and gas power plants.

State and federal government provide tax credits and other programs that support individuals owning their own electricity power plants. That includes their RV or boat! While there are cases for grid based electrical generation and transmission, why not go solar if you can? Helping the environment heal is a good reason to go renewable by itself. Additionally, if most residences and businesses were independently powered, terrorism targeting infrastructure would become much less effective. War-mongering countries would not be able to hold peace loving countries hostage over oil and gas prices. Power and coal companies won't support renewable energy, nor will the politicians they lobby. Finally, once you make the investment in solar, you don't have to be concerned about electric utility companies raising the rates. If you have an interconnect with the electric utility grid and sell power you aren't using, the rate they pay you could go up. I believe it is up to citizens to make this world better by installing their own renewable energy sources. We the people can leverage our buying power and force corporations to manufacture what we want and need in the most environmentally conscious way. Finally, consider a vision of a dark, pollution cloaked, dead world full of fossil-fueled machines trying to clean the air while pumping tons of carbon dioxide into the ground. Now consider a world in harmony with nature, filled with bright sunlight, and clean air, where you can hear birds singing and watch the butterflies, a scene of peace with solar panels on every house, and every home and vacant lot with a garden. Which world do you want to live in?

CHAPTER 39:
TINY HOMES ON
THE WATER

When I made my decision to pursue this project, there was a lot of fear and uncertainty in the world because of the Covid-19 pandemic. People were drinking bleach and taking animal antibiotics to fight the virus. So many people were getting ill that there weren't enough hospital beds and doctors to treat them. Funeral homes were running out of places to store the bodies of those who succumbed to the illness. There were online battles between people promoting theories about the disease, promulgating bizarre cures for it, and those publishing truth and facts. In my past life, between working 50 hours a week and being on call the rest of the time, I rarely read or watched the news. That all changed for me after losing my job. When the pandemic hit, I spent hours reading news stories. Craziness swept the world. There were demonstrations, people shooting other people; riots and vandalism were rampant. The weather was becoming wilder due to climate change. Not to mention the environment was becoming more toxic with chemical spills, microplastics, and pollution. I felt useless, knowing that the world was changing for the worse, and there wasn't anything I could do to help make it better. So, I decided to go to work and strive to be the change in the world I wanted to see. I couldn't actualize my wildest dreams, but I had enough money put aside to accomplish my goal of turning my boat into an off-the-grid tiny home. I parlayed $25,000 into a lifestyle with 10-million-dollar views, no homeowners' associations, no mortgage, and no property taxes. Now I only pay for boat licensing and registration (which includes an excise tax), liability insurance, and for moorage at a marina if I need to stay somewhere for a while. If I want to change my scenery, I can easily cast off from the dock or pull up the anchor and move somewhere else. No utilities to contact, no background checks, no leases to sign, and no boxes to pack. I meet new people all the time and have had some great adventures. I am of retirement age, but because of my new lifestyle, I get a lot of exercise. I haven't felt healthier in years, and I hope to be able to sail to some exotic locations in the future. It also occurred to me, by living in this boat, I am also freeing up housing where others could live. It's no secret that the population of Washington and other states is increasing. Homes are becoming so expensive that most people can't afford to buy them, and the number of homeless people is growing. Most boats built since 1960 are made of fiberglass, and sturdy enough to withstand the harsh marine environment. Many old boats can be refurbished economically to serve another lifetime as tiny homes, either on the water or on land. I hope this book will help you decide if you want to take on a project like this. If you do, I hope it will give you incentive, save you some time, money, and aggravation. It will be worth it.

CHAPTER 40: FINISHING THOUGHTS AND QUOTES

I wrote this book because I wanted to demonstrate that it is possible for individuals to make a difference. People can make their own electricity and in doing so, reduce greenhouse gases. People can build and live in affordable homes on the water. I believe that awareness and concern for the environment will increase as people take to living on the water as a lifestyle. I hope that they will organize and influence the state and local government to legislate in favor of liveaboard communities. I hope that people who read this book will influence and educate others who may then eschew pouring fossil fuels into water sports. For each motorized water sport, there is an environmentally conscious one just as fun. I confess that I have bias for anything that helps the environment. This feeling has grown during my experiences while sailing my boat around Puget Sound. So has my appreciation of nature around us. I hope that humanity can change its course and build a more sustainable tomorrow.

Here are some inspirational quotes from famous people:

"Never doubt that a small group of thoughtful committed citizens can change the world; indeed, it's the only thing that ever has". Margaret Mead

"Be the Change You Wish to See in the World". This quote is attributed to Arleen Lorrance. Mohandas Gandhi also said something along those lines.

EPILOGUE

Something interesting happened while I was finishing this book, so I am taking the opportunity to address it. When living on a boat, whether at sea or docked at a marina, you need a physical address for your car insurance, driver's license, and other things. I use a U.S. Post Office box to receive mail. In the past, because I had a liveaboard contract with the marina, I used my marina's address and slip number as my physical address. When I moved to the Olympia area, I had to go on a waiting list for liveaboard privileges. I went to the post office in Olympia to open a new PO box for my mail and spoke to a post office employee regarding a physical address. She said I could use the post office address with my PO box number as the unit number for that. It was my legal physical address. This was fine when updating my auto insurance and driver's license. In Washington, when you update your driver's license, you can also request to have your information sent to the appropriate county auditor's office to update your voter's registration. I did, and a few weeks later, I received letters from Tacoma's Pierce County and Olympia's Thurston County informing me that they couldn't use the Post Office location as my physical address for voting purposes. I went online to verify my address was correct. It was. Then, one day I got a call from the Thurston County Auditor's office. I had a conversation with the employee, who told me that the Post Office was considered a business and couldn't be used. I told her about my residence aboard my sailboat and told her about my conversation with the post office and asked her if she had any ideas. She said I could use my new marina's address and the slip number where I moored my boat.

She entered that in the computer, and it was accepted. I was a little confused because the marina was a business, too. I asked her how homeless people voted if they didn't have a physical address and couldn't use the post office address. She said the way around that was to use the address from the street corner they usually hung out at. The reason I wrote this paragraph is to let you know that liveaboards and homeless people have a physical address and can always register to vote. I encourage everybody to participate in our democracy!

Made in the USA
Middletown, DE
13 July 2024

57254676R00088